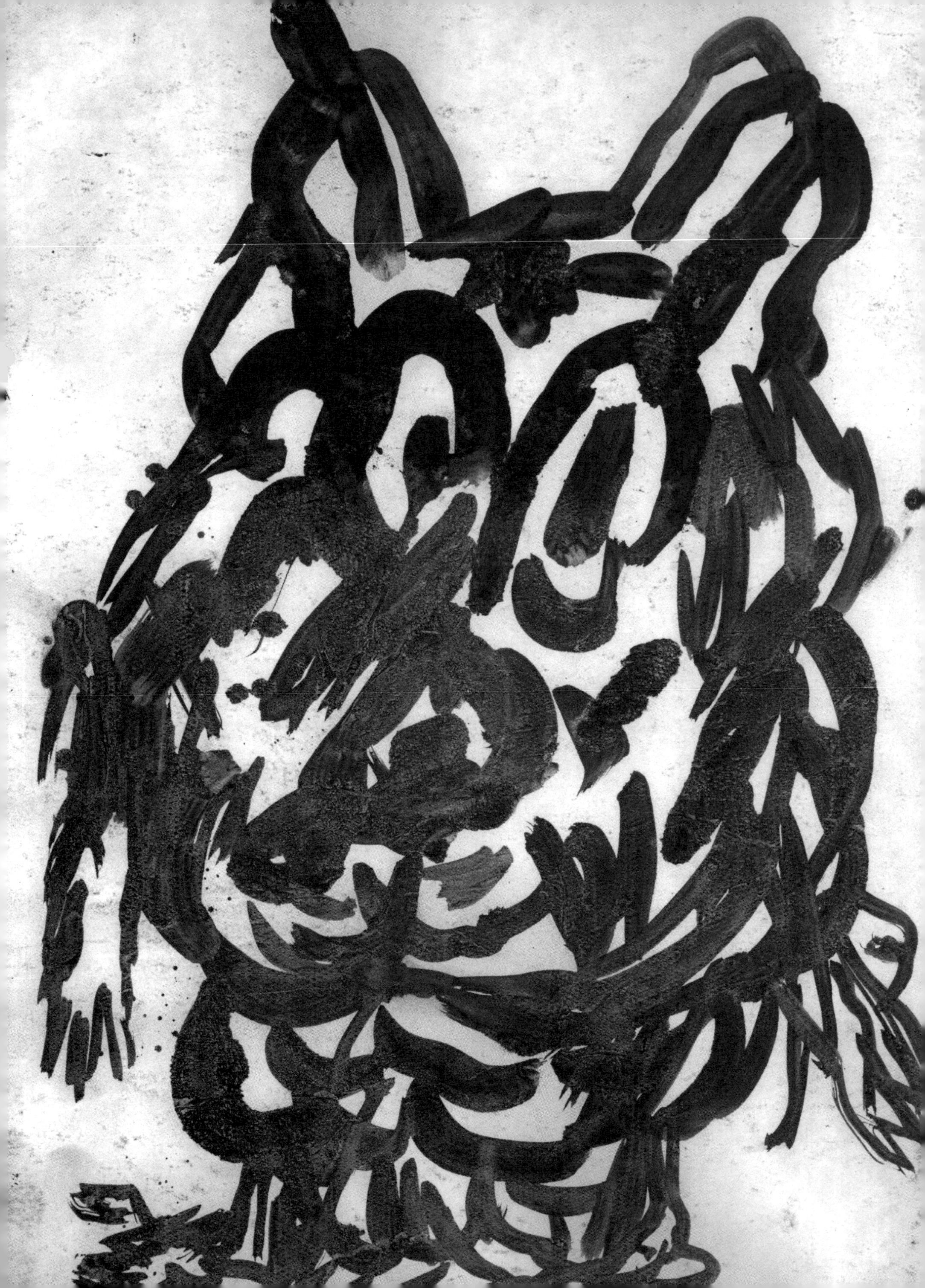

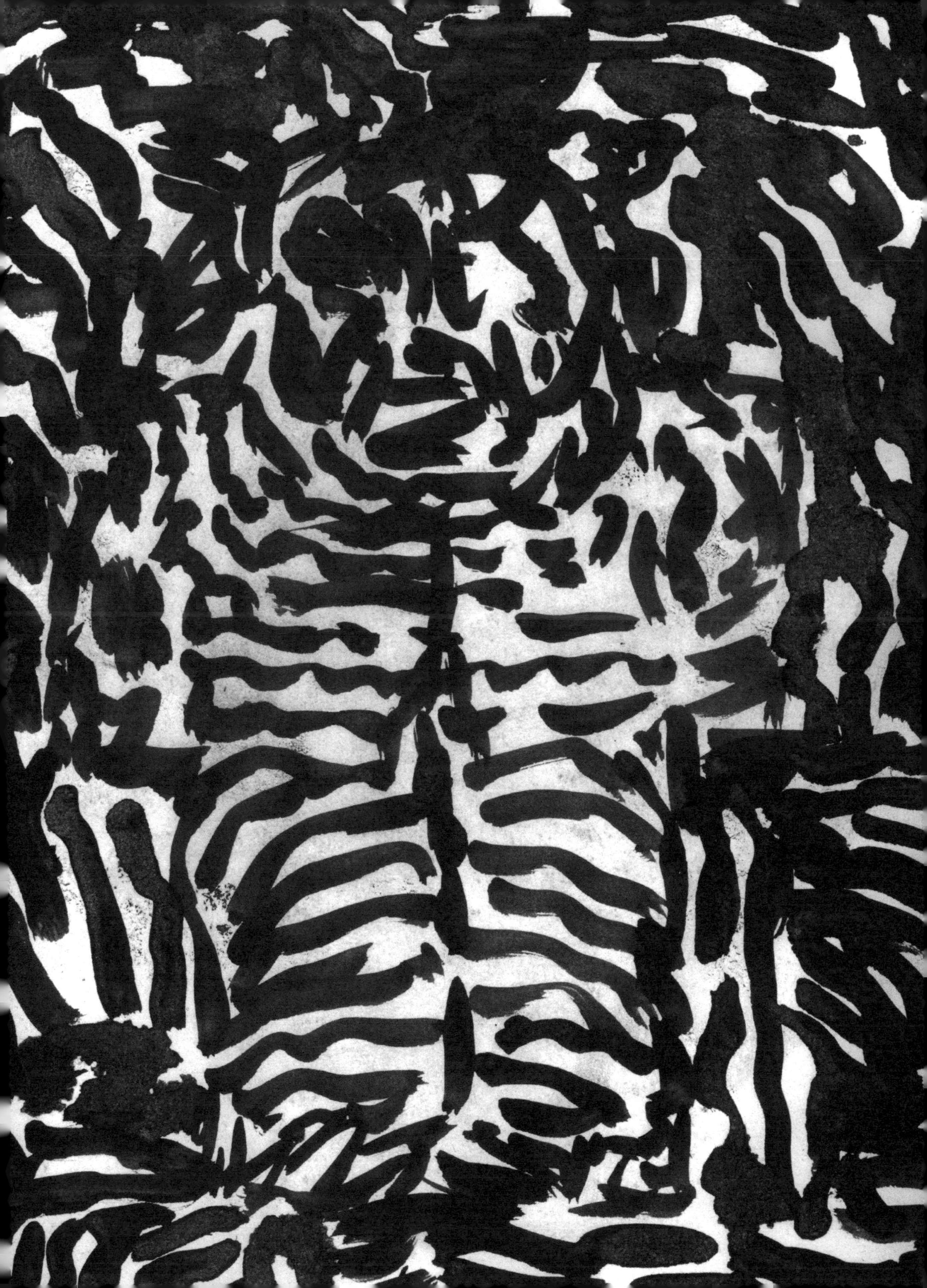

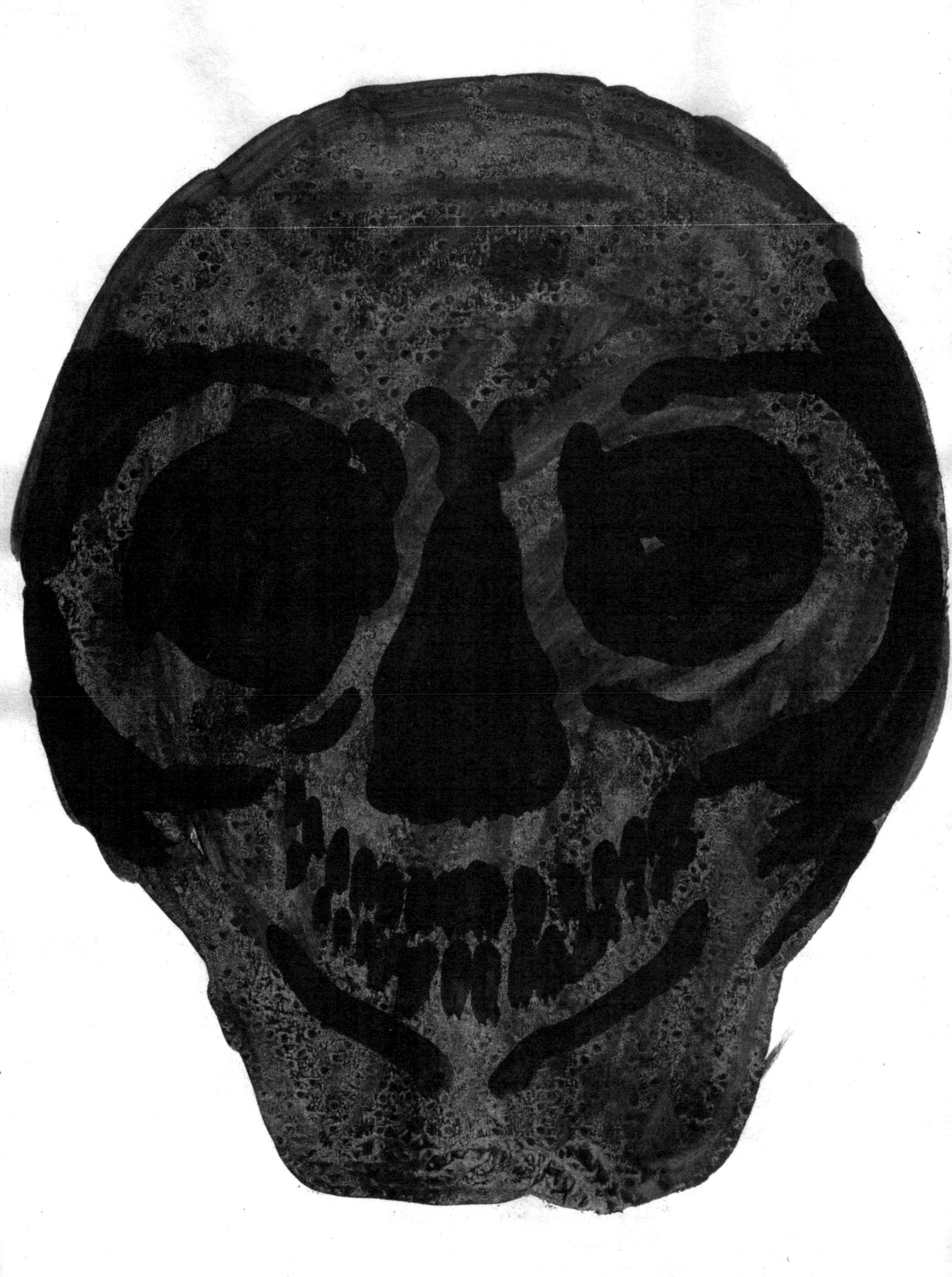

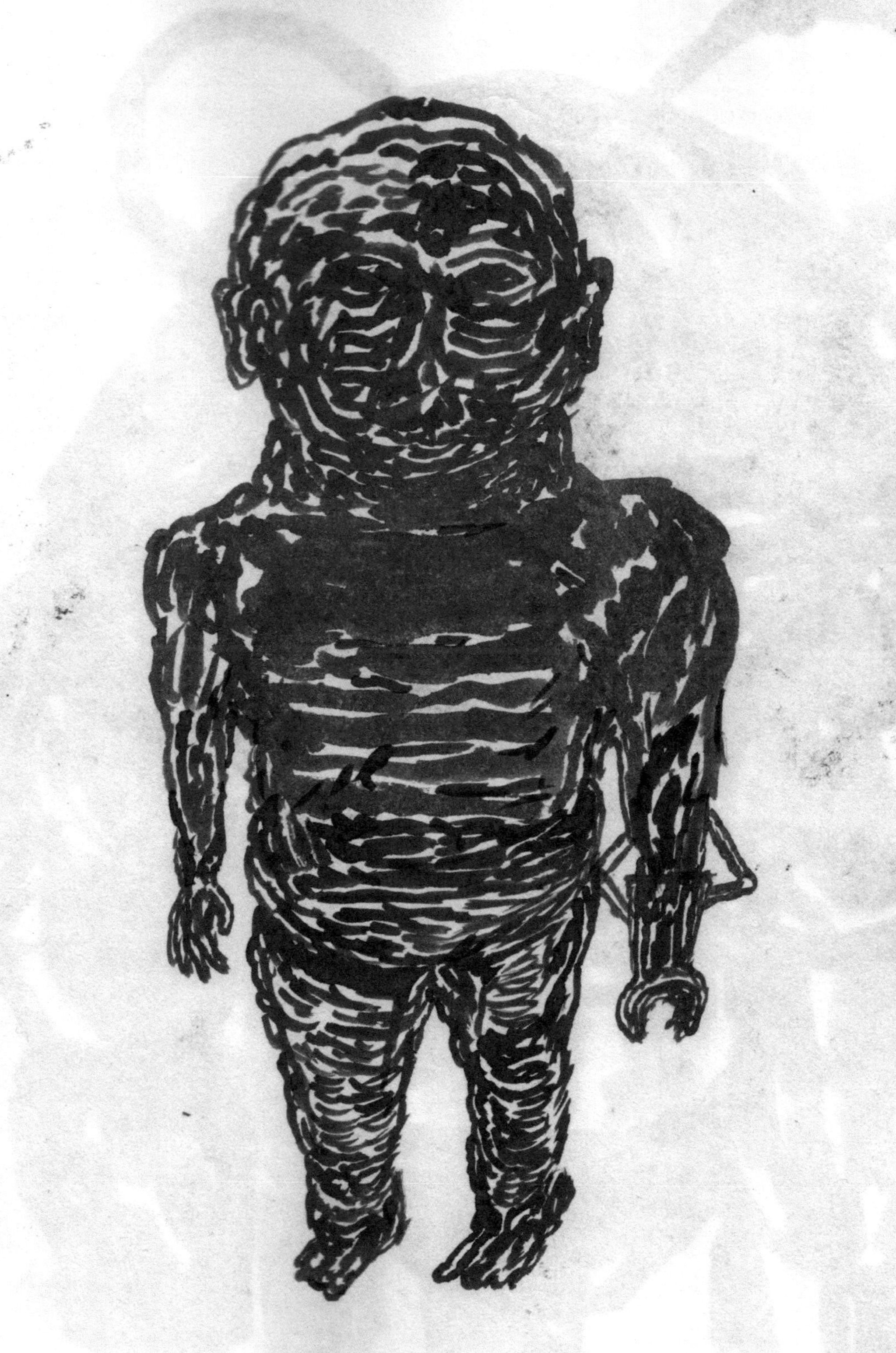

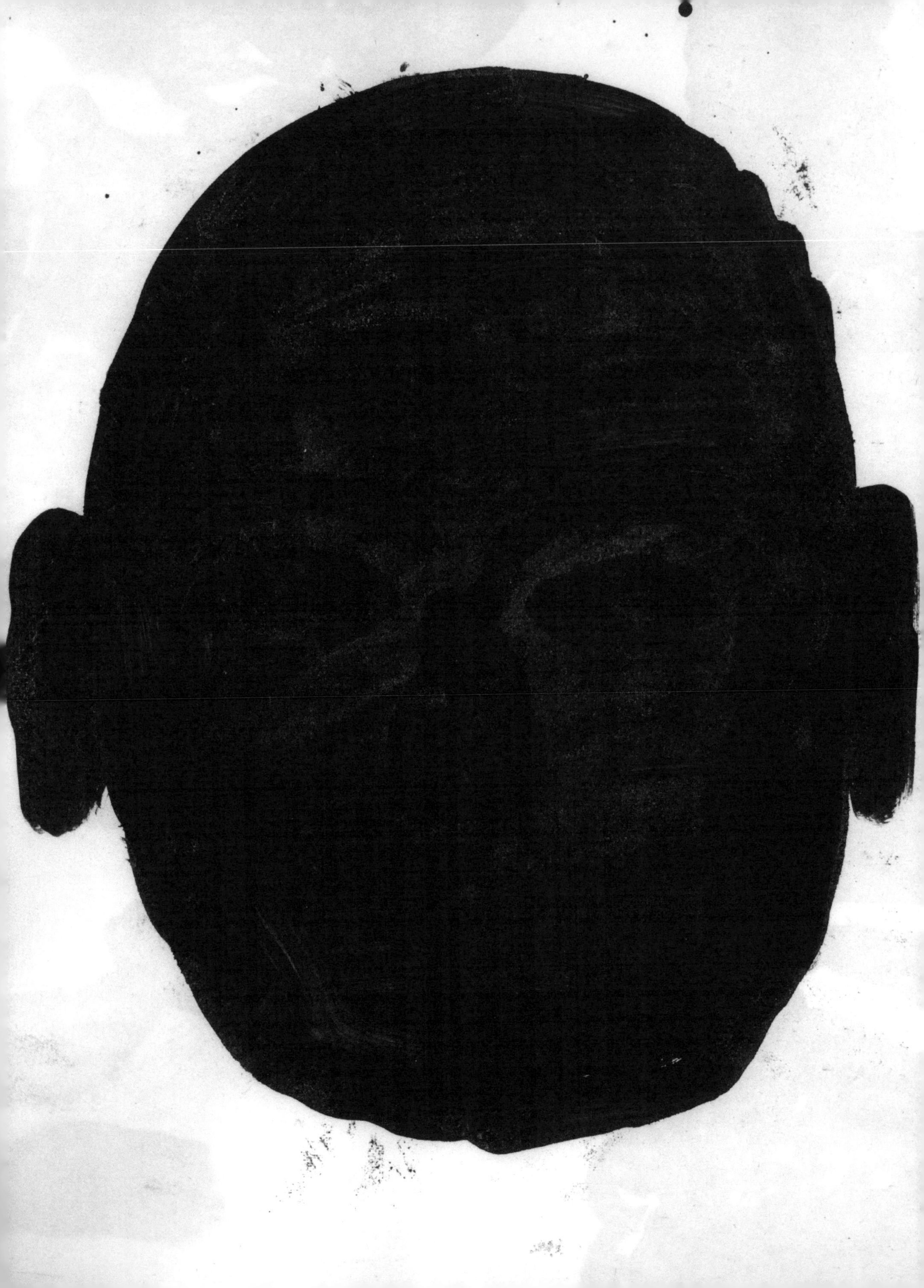

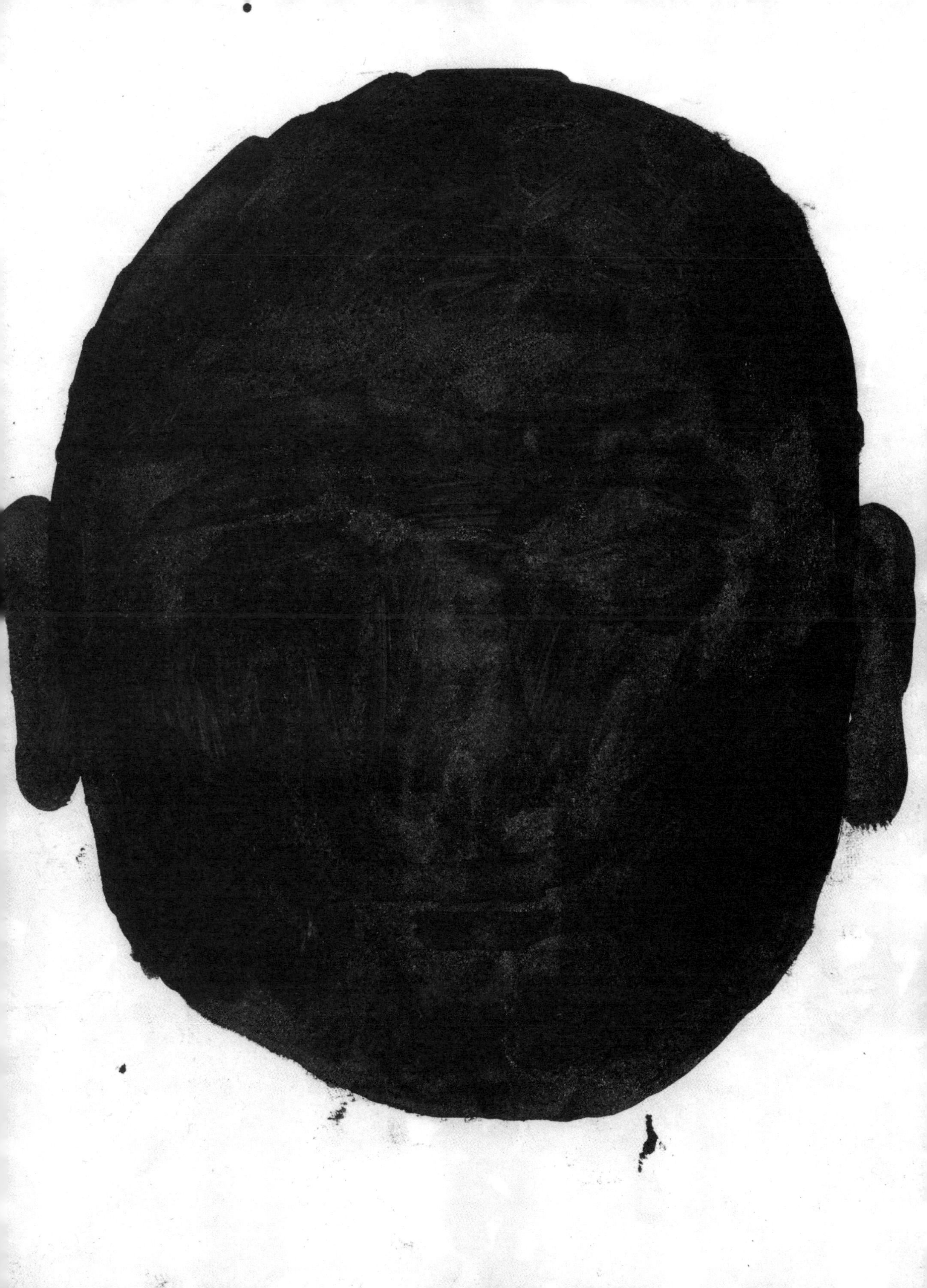

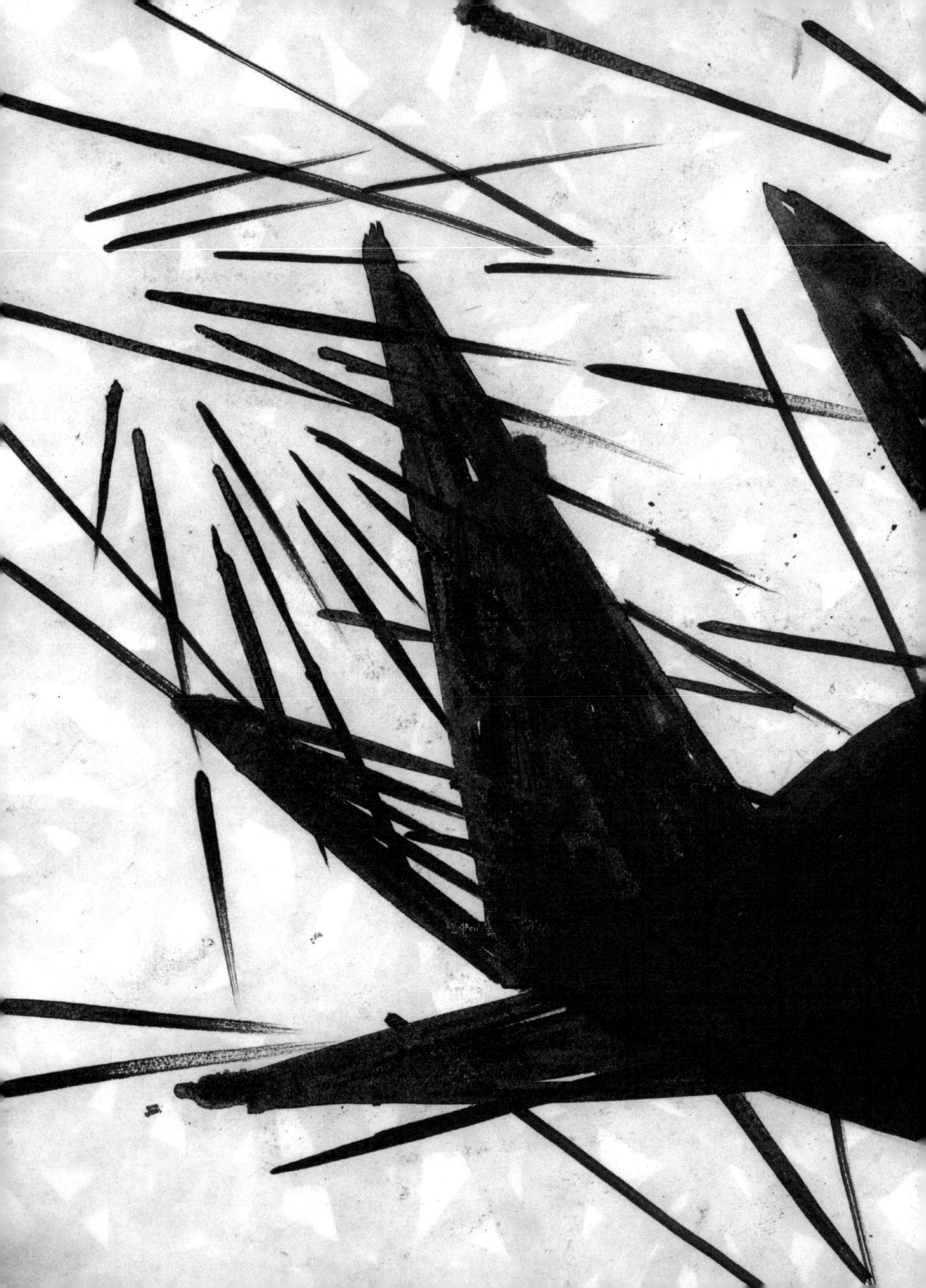

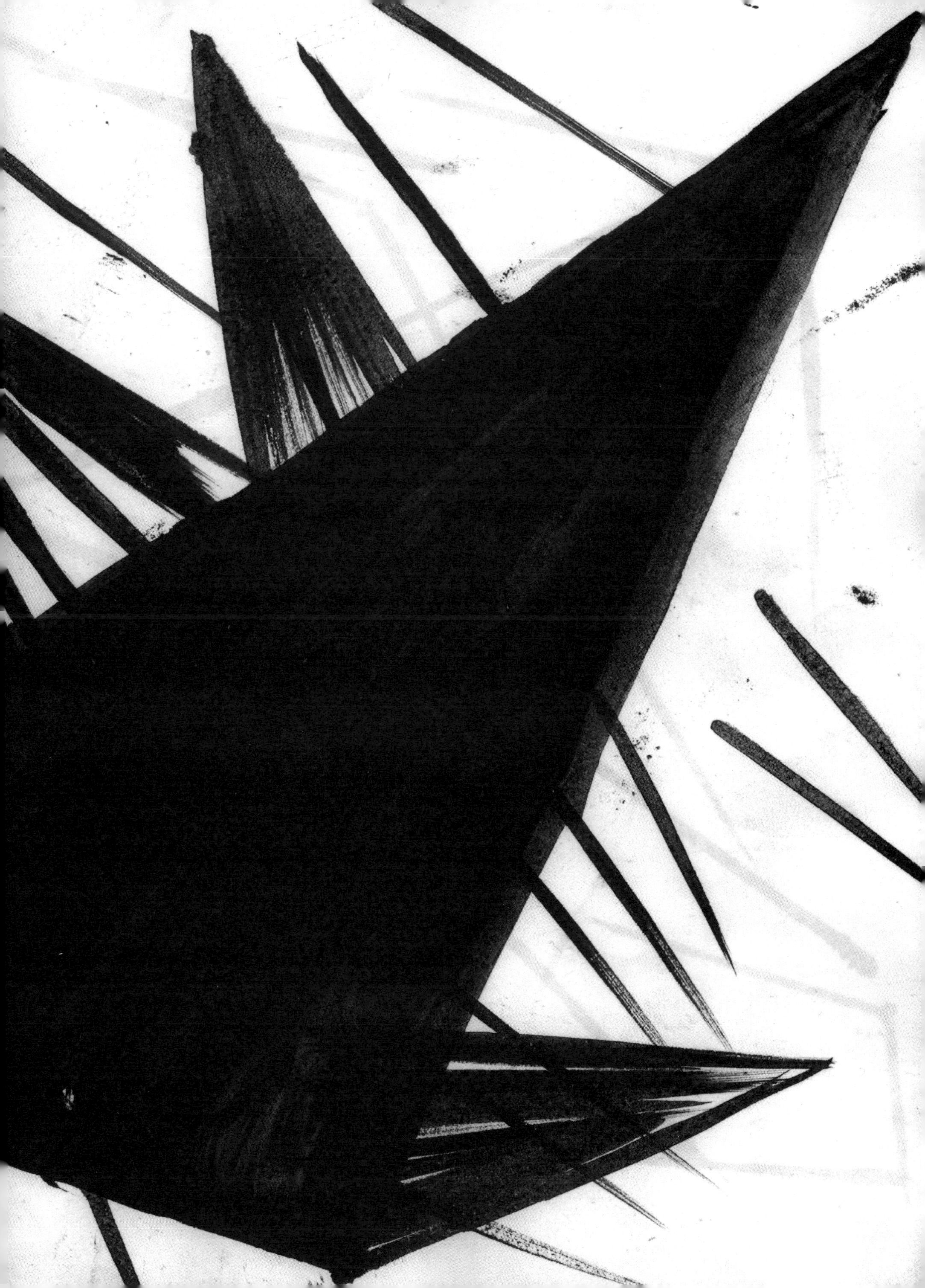

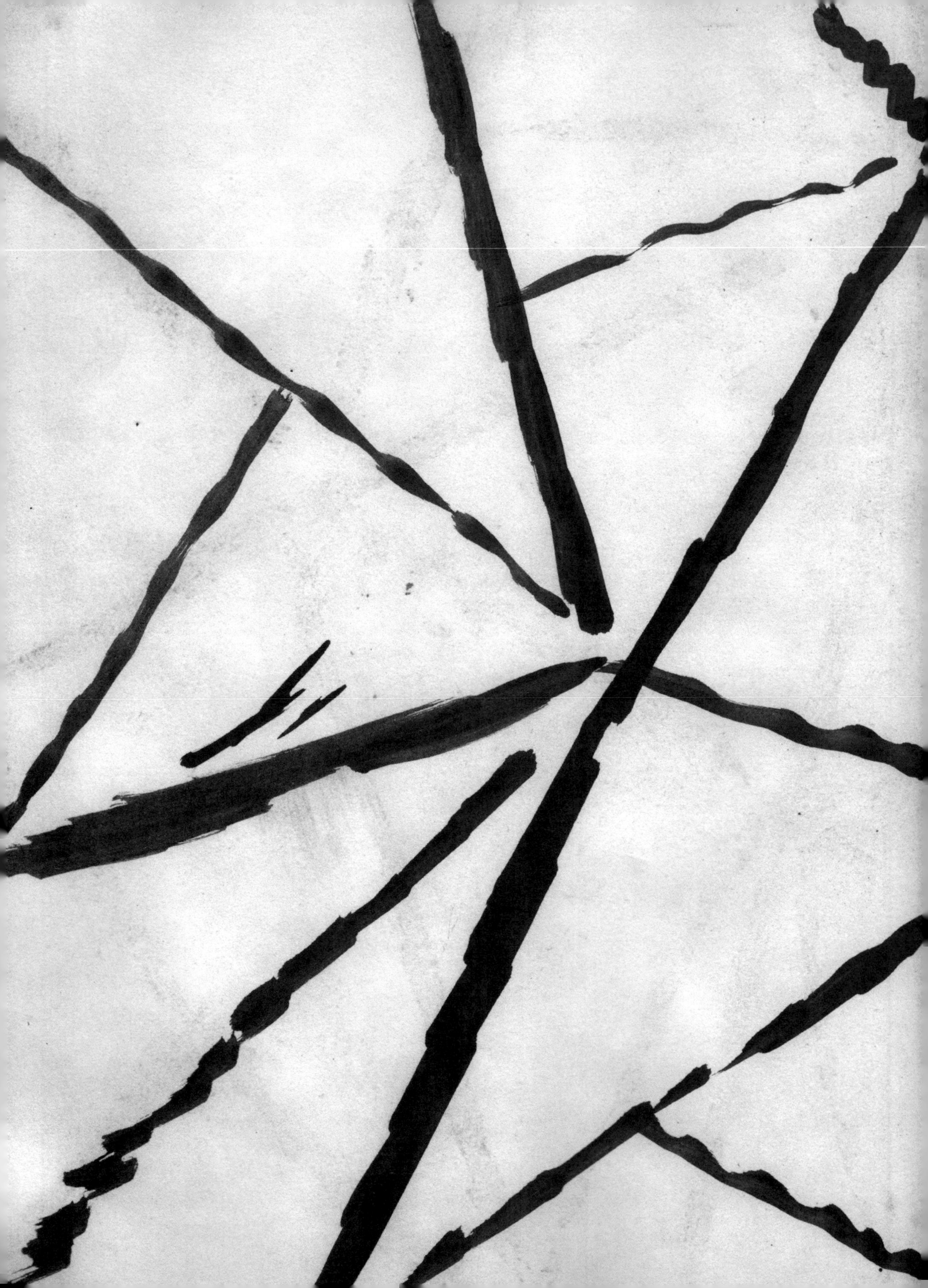

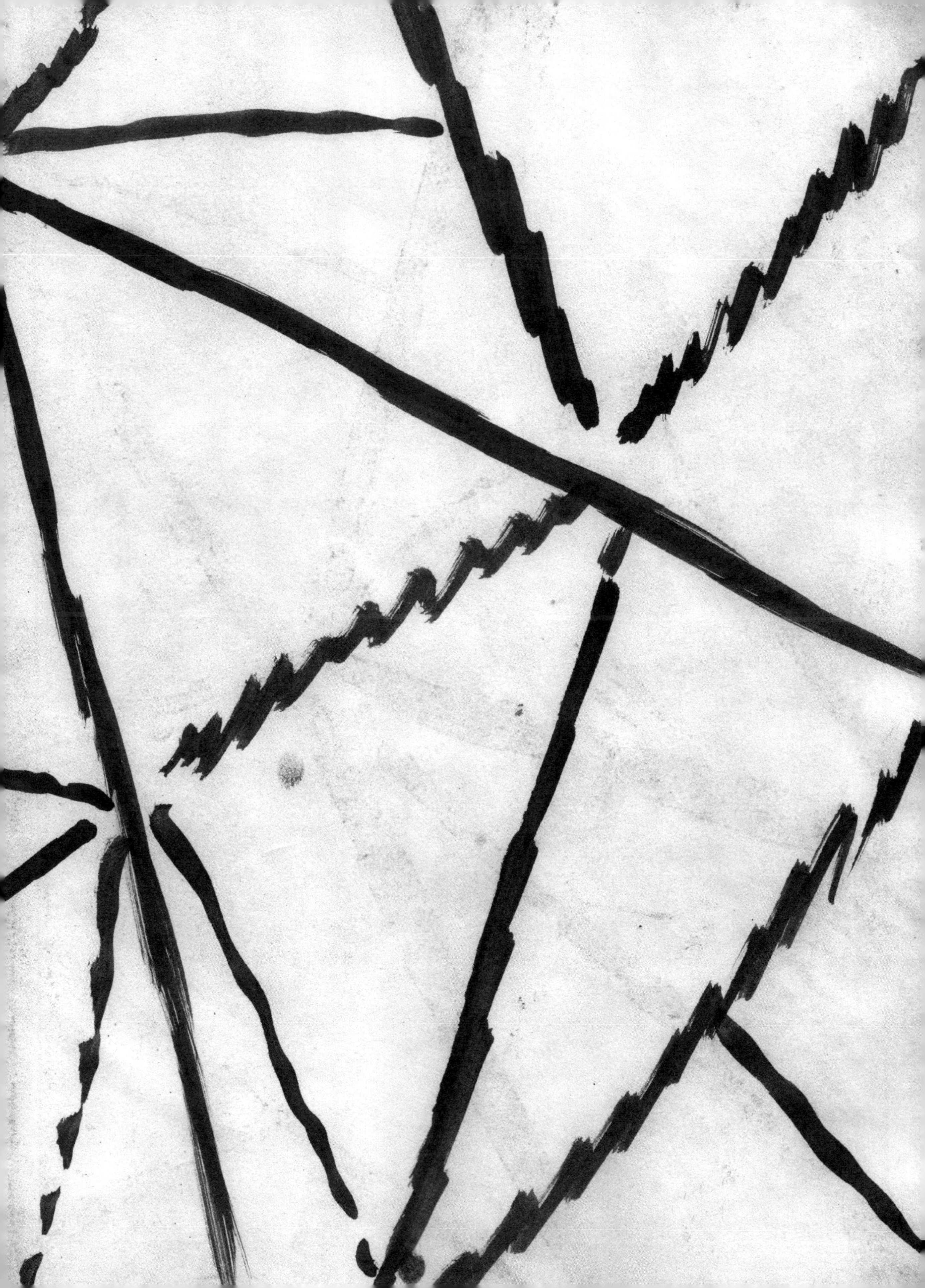

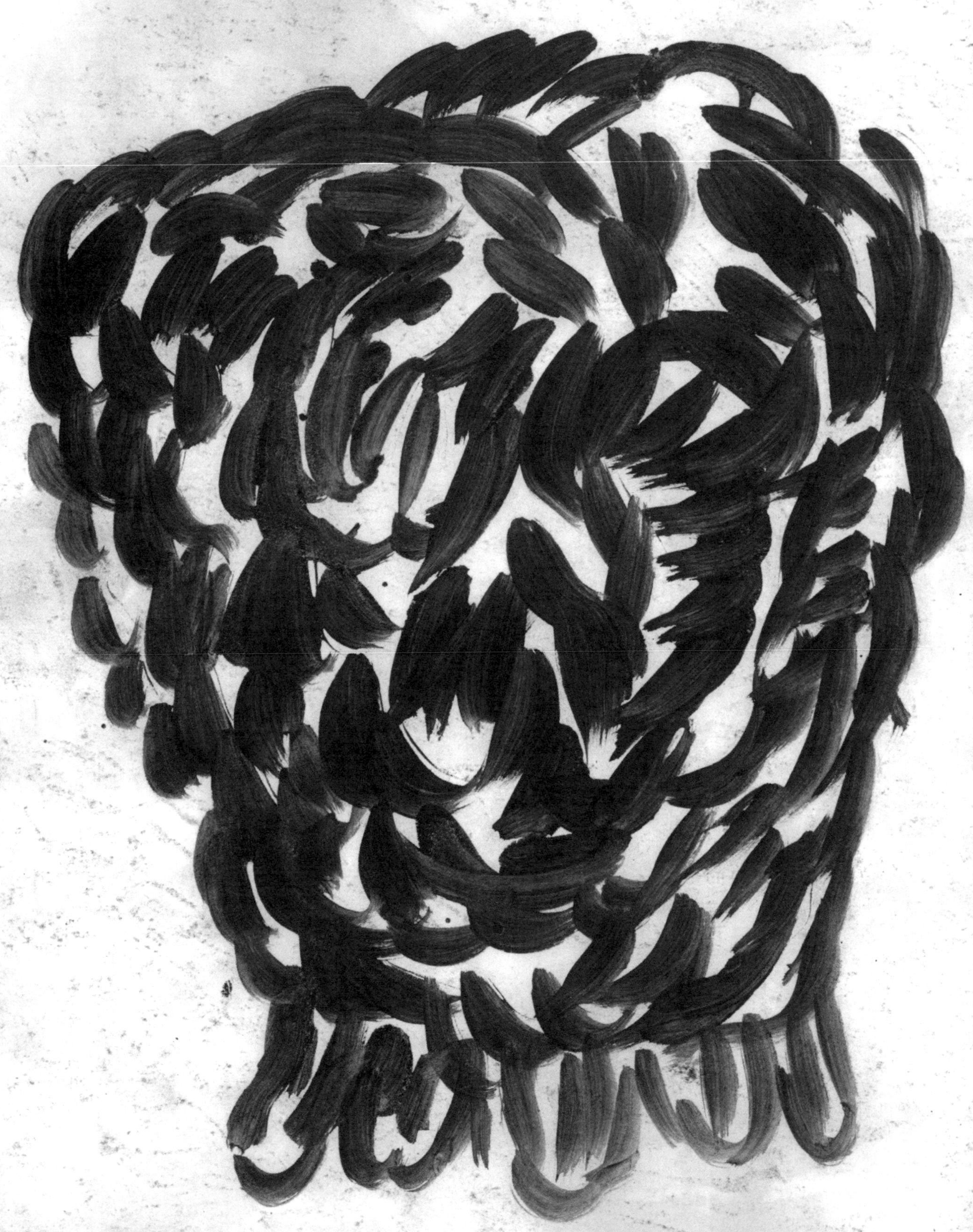

While the oil tries to reach the
snake's head, it's legs become
completely encoiled

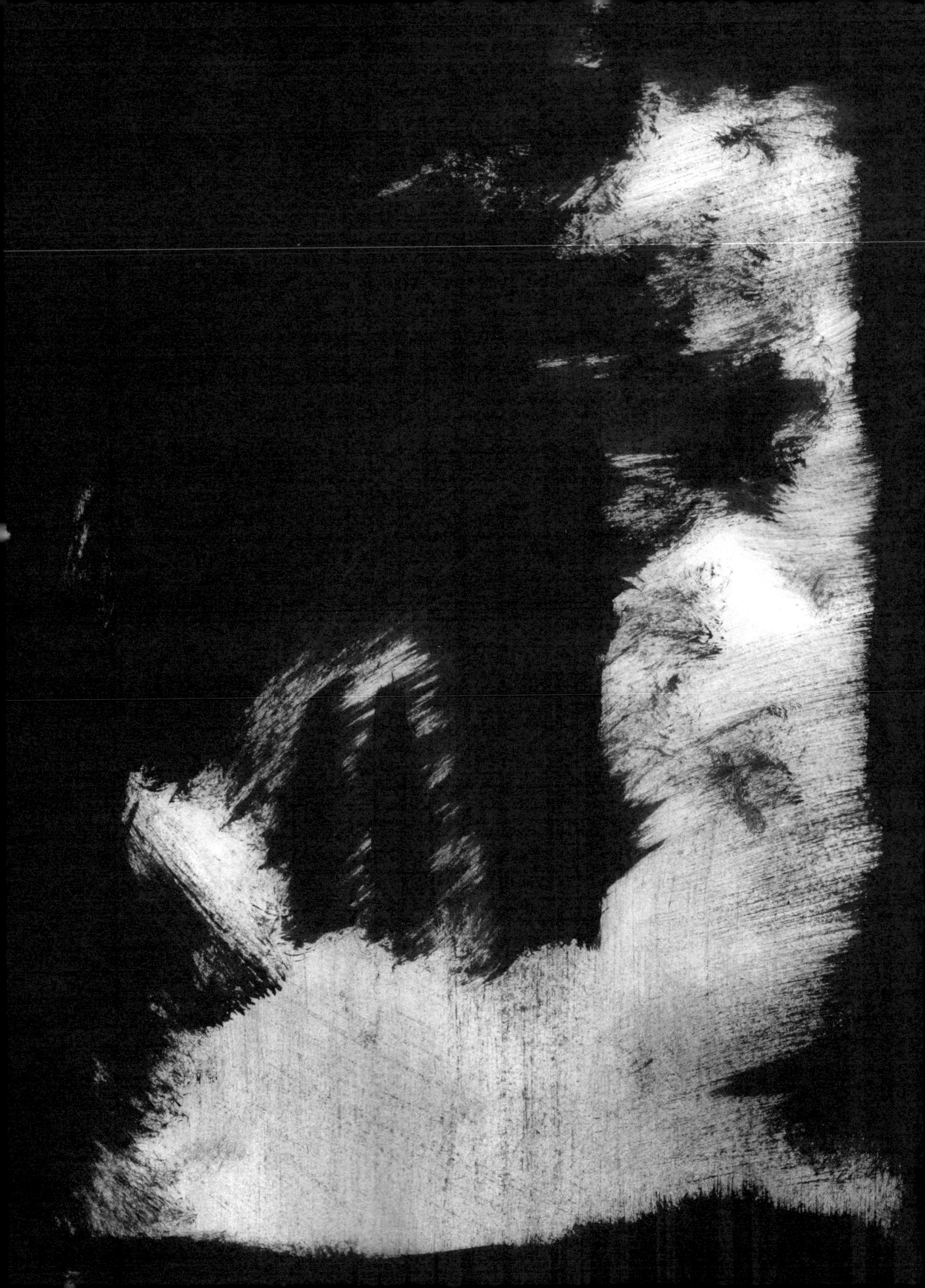

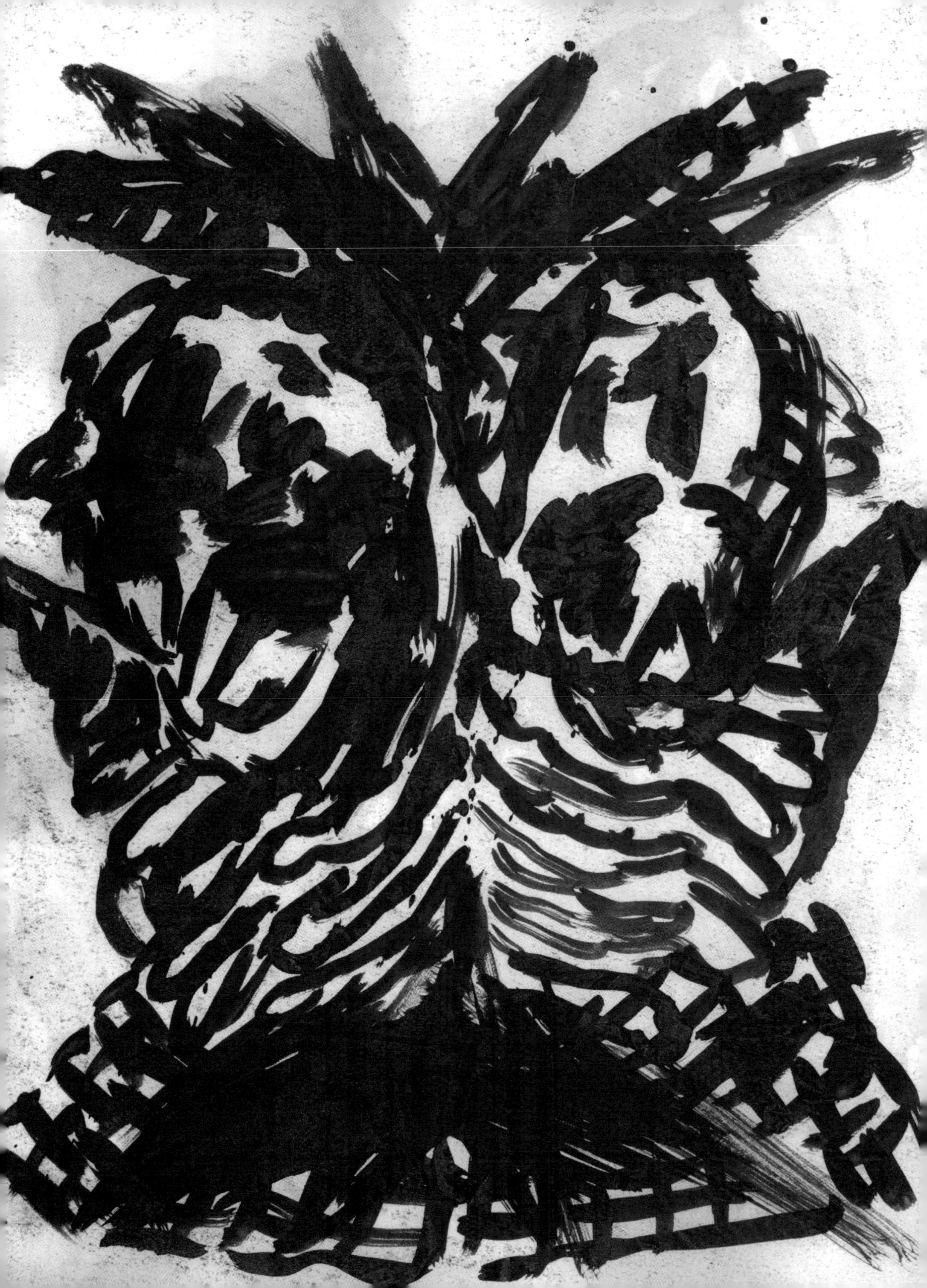

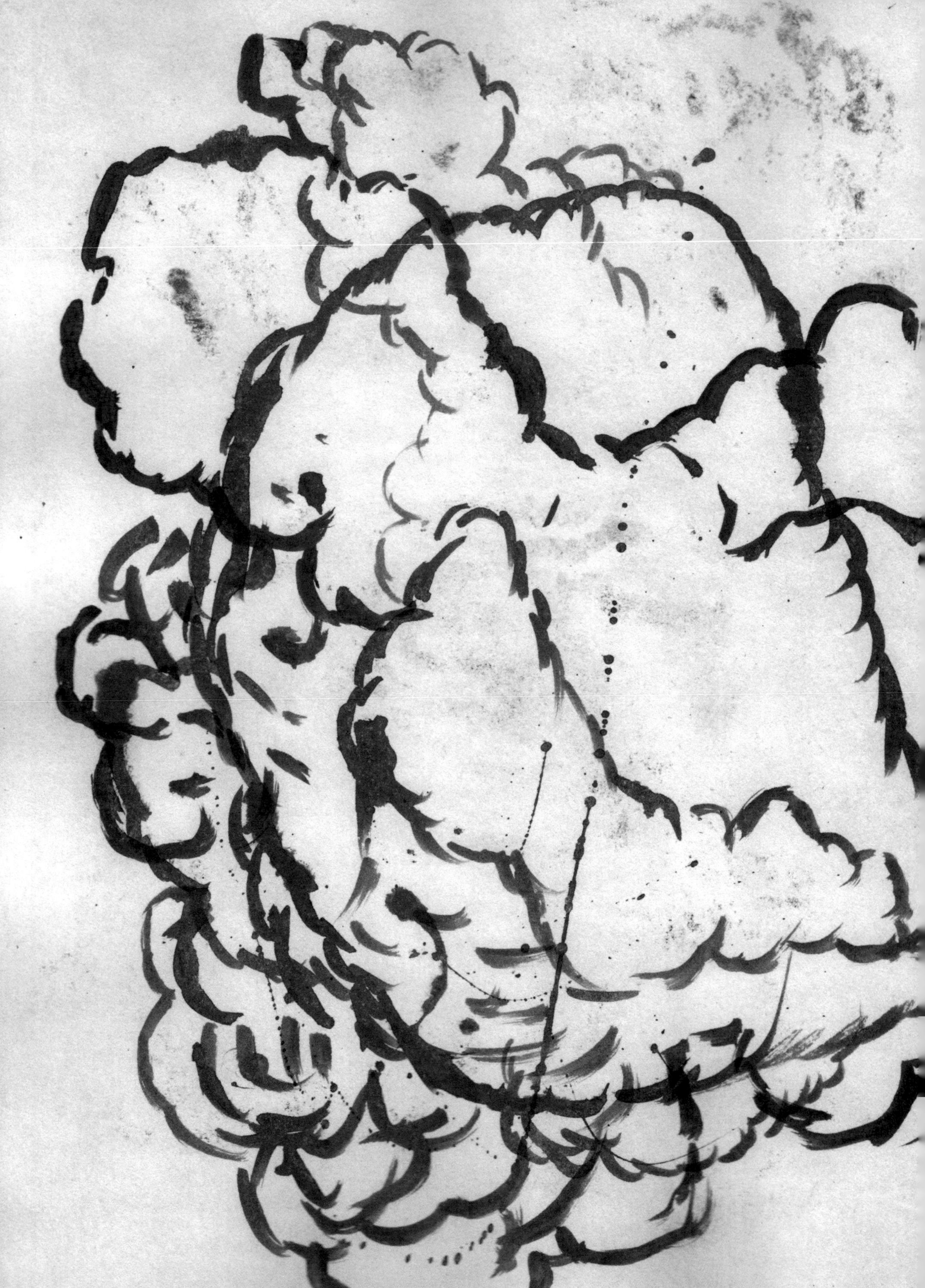

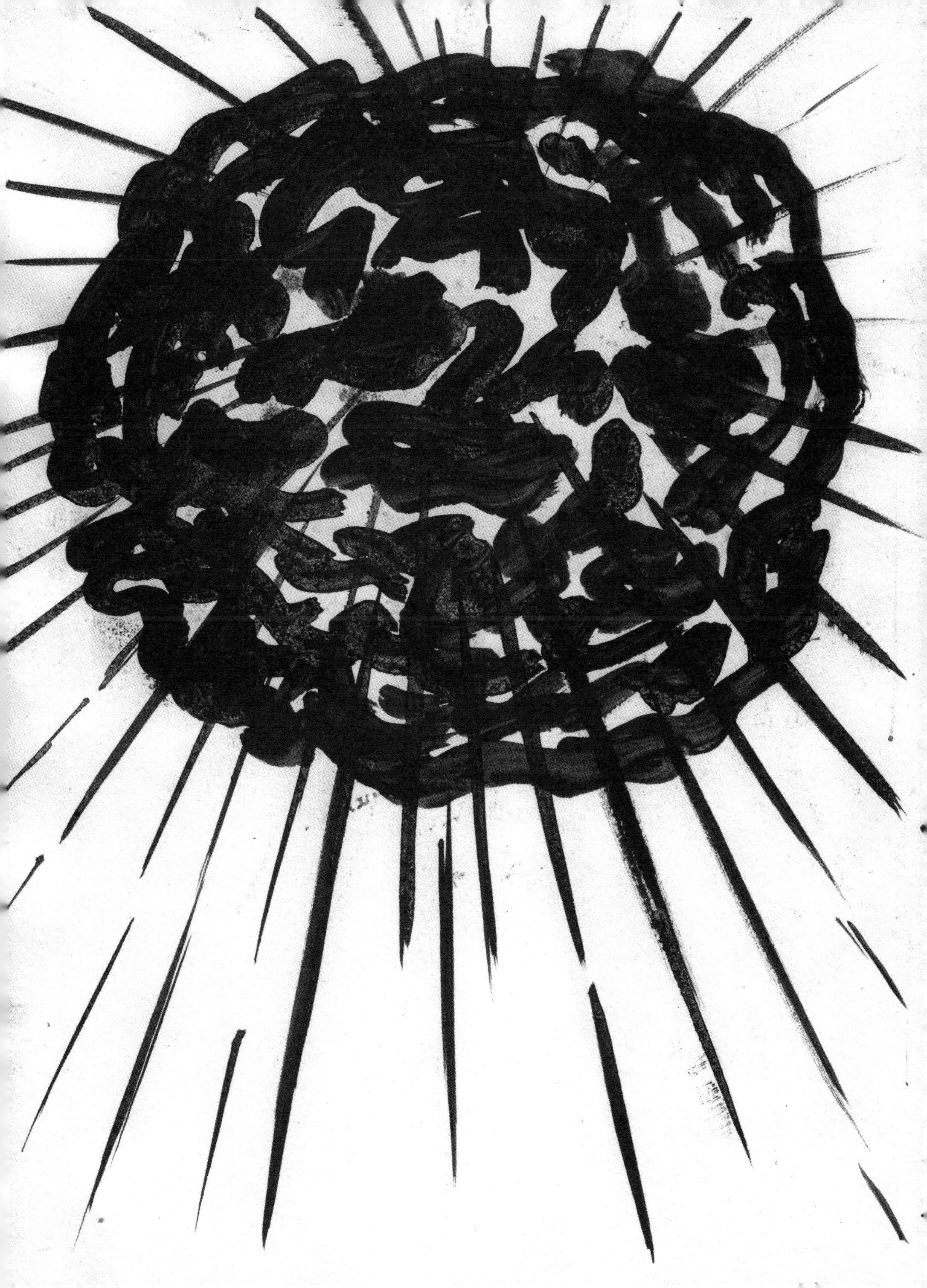

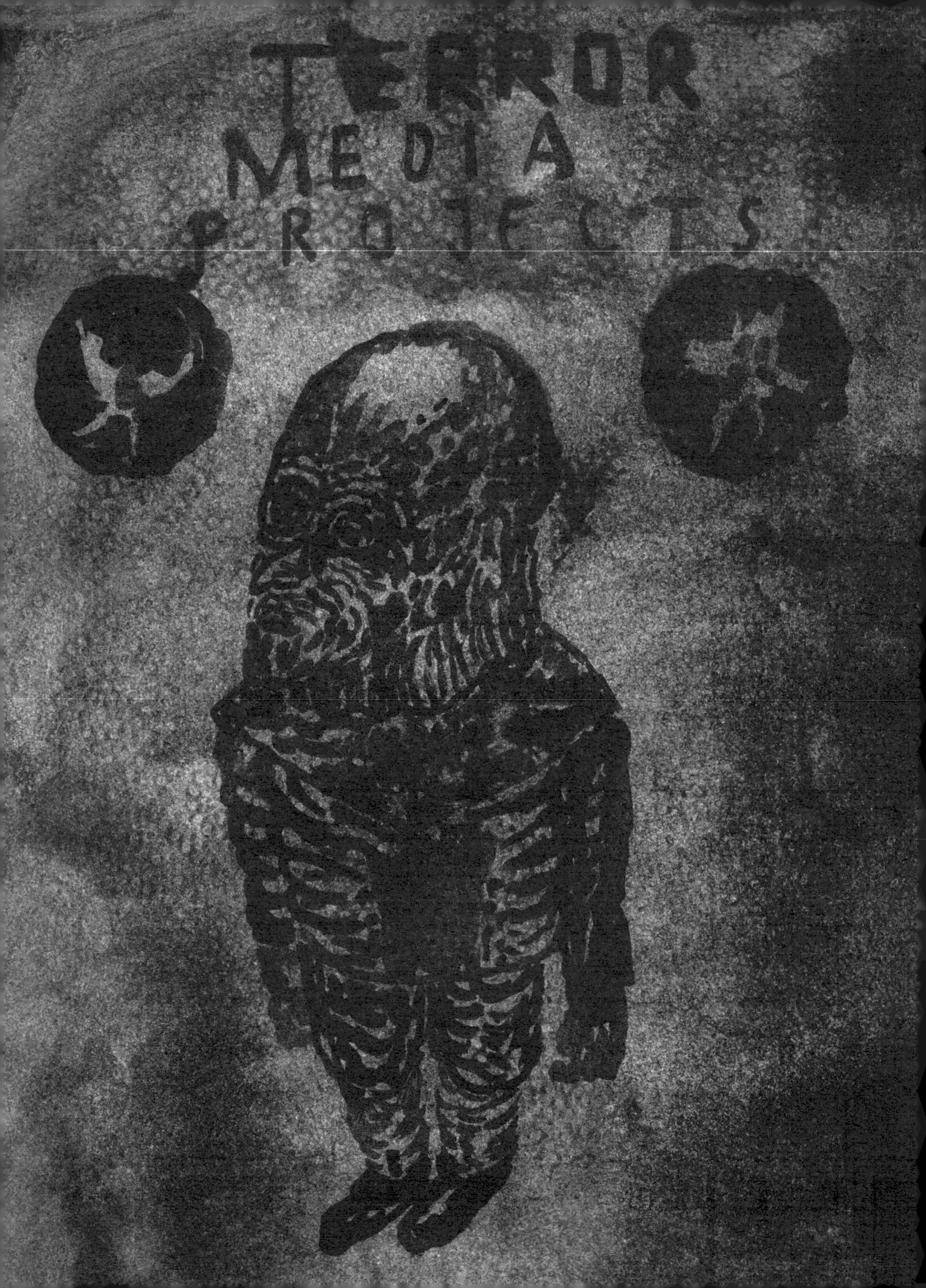
TERROR
MEDIA
PROJECTS

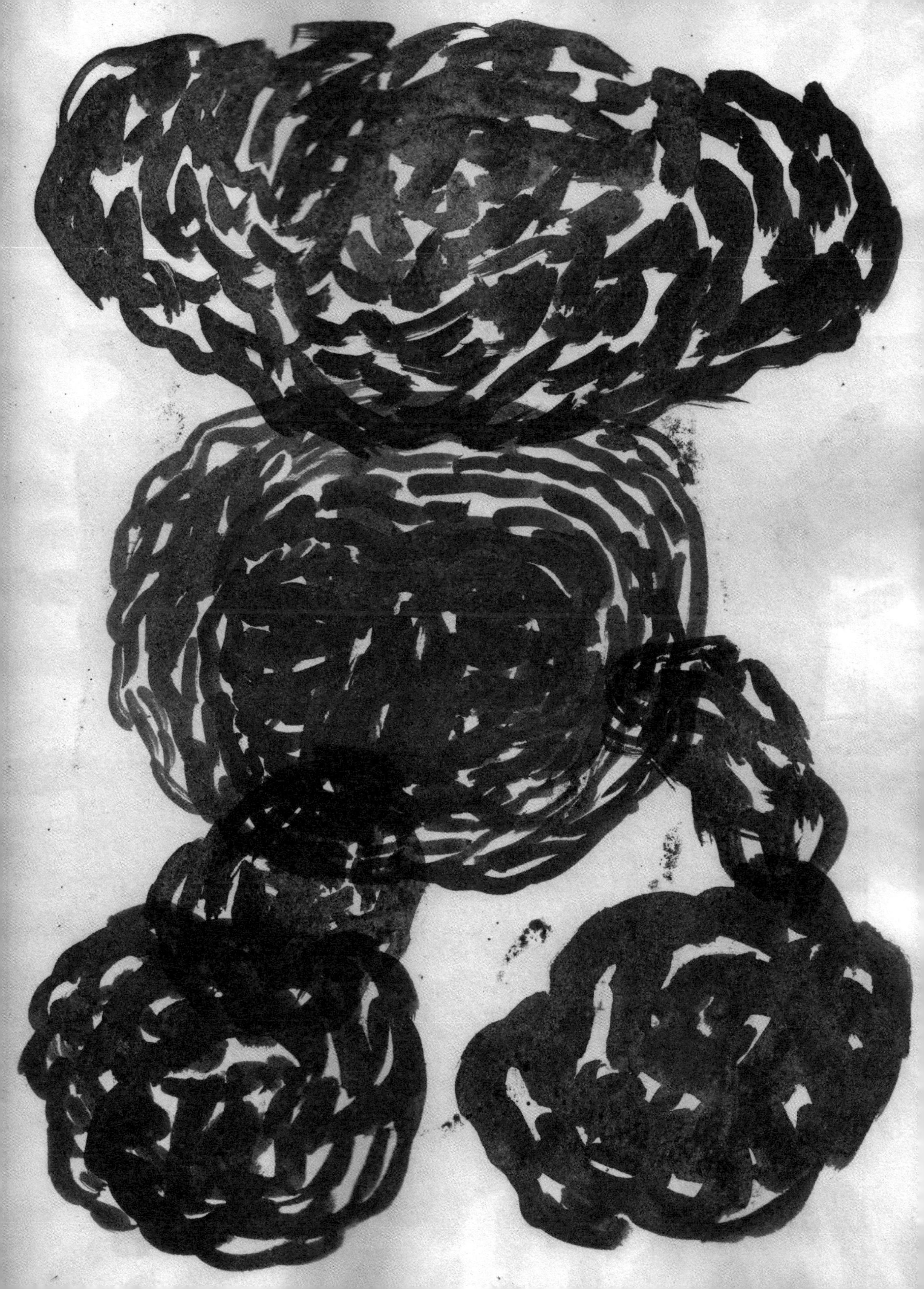

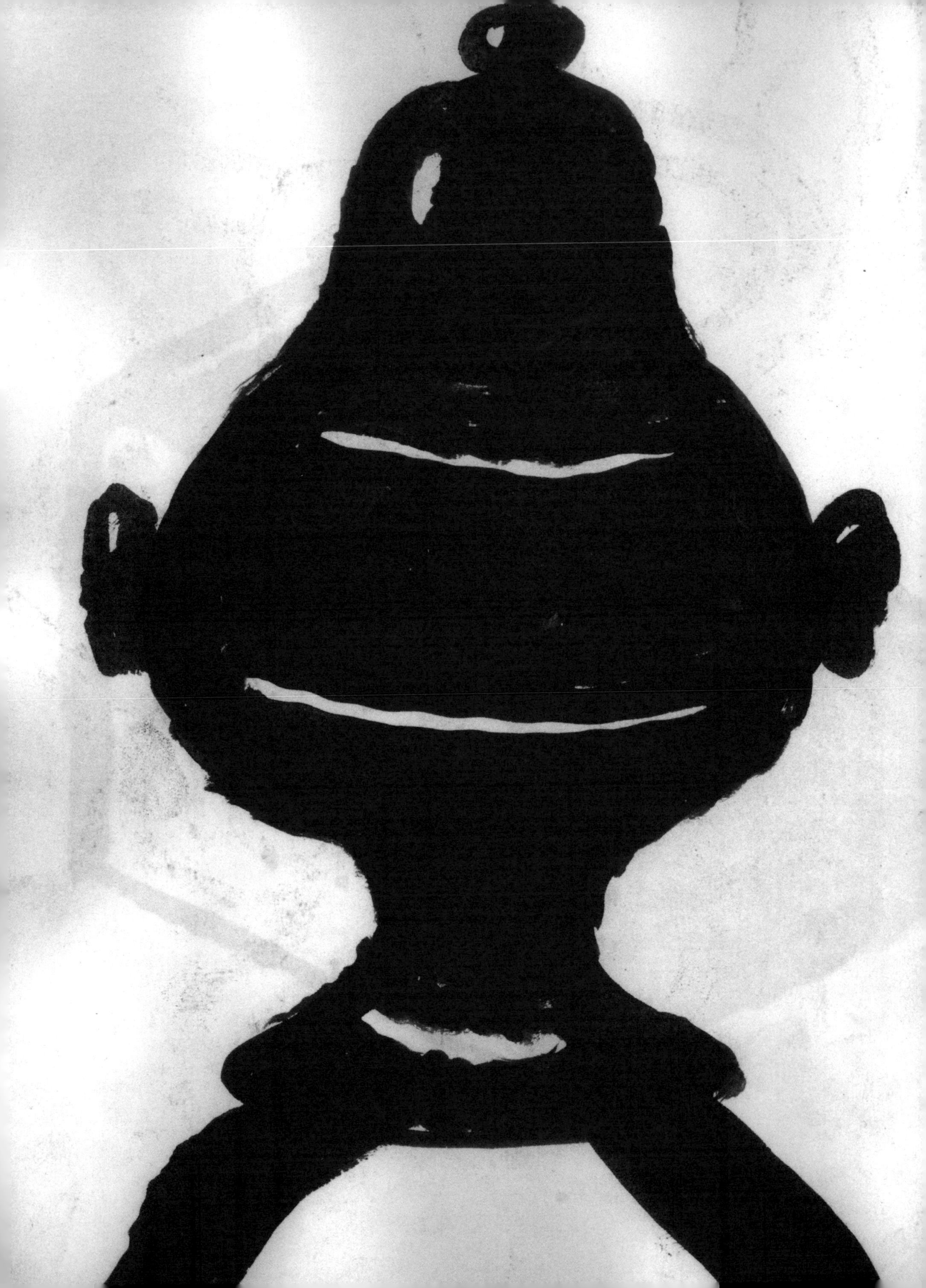

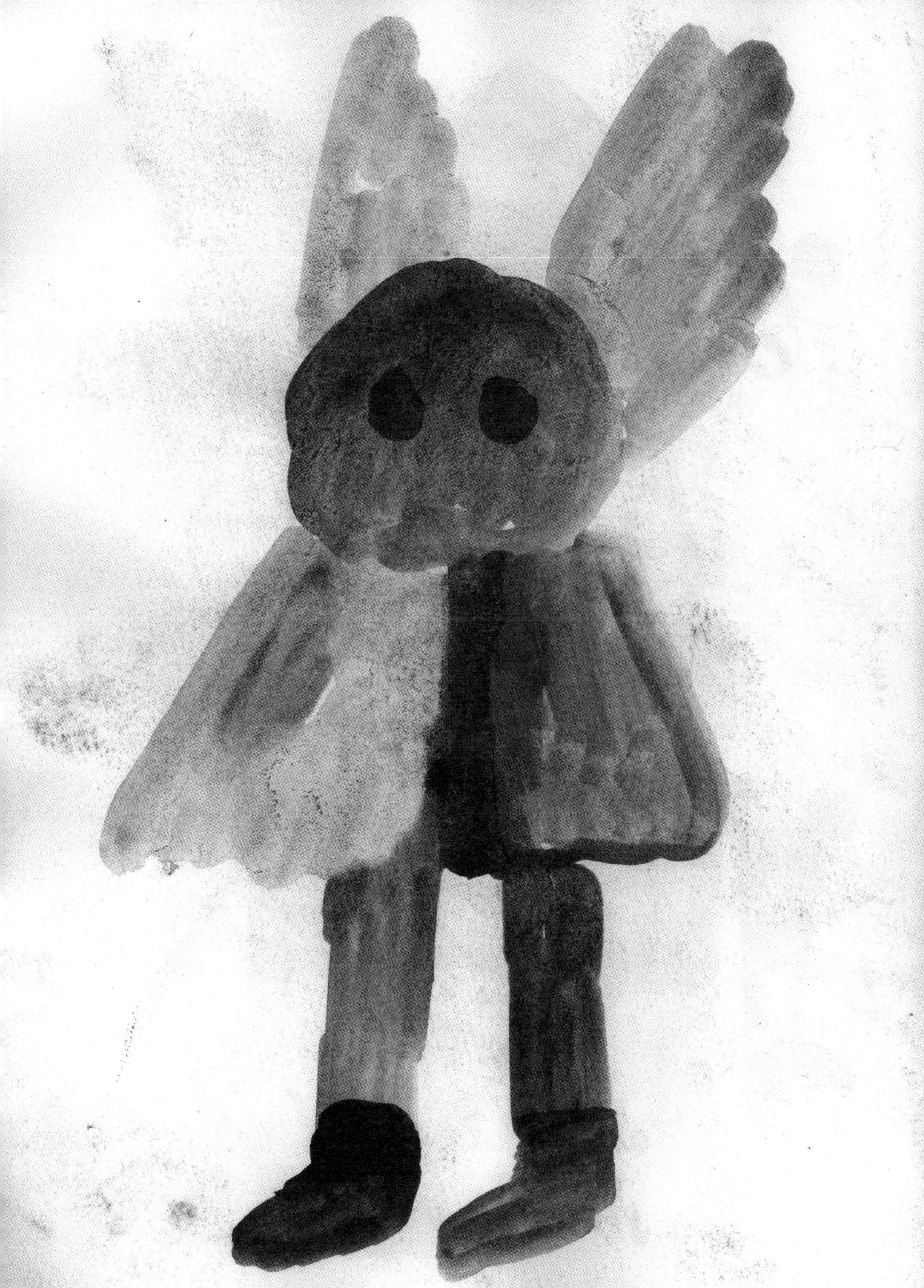

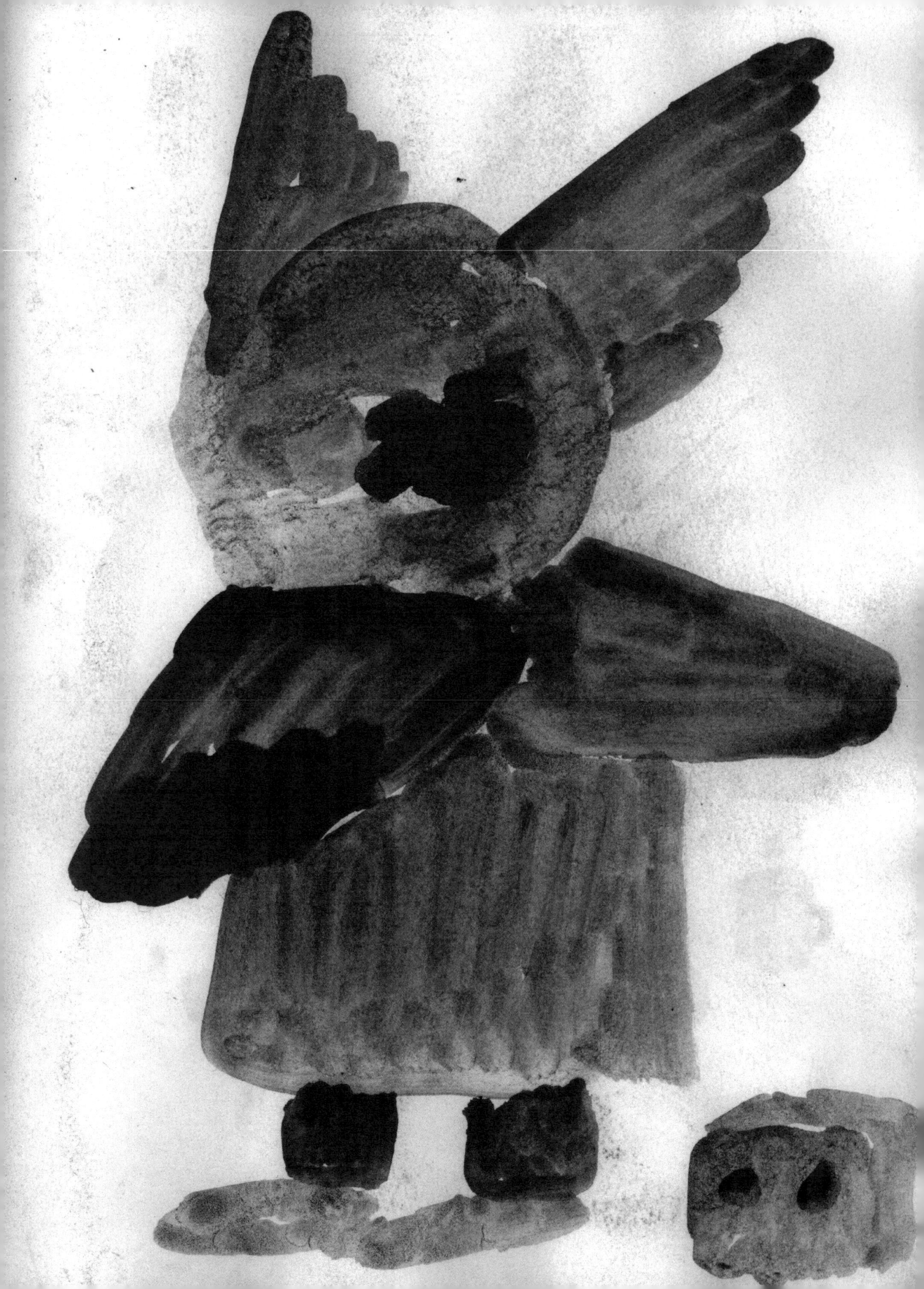

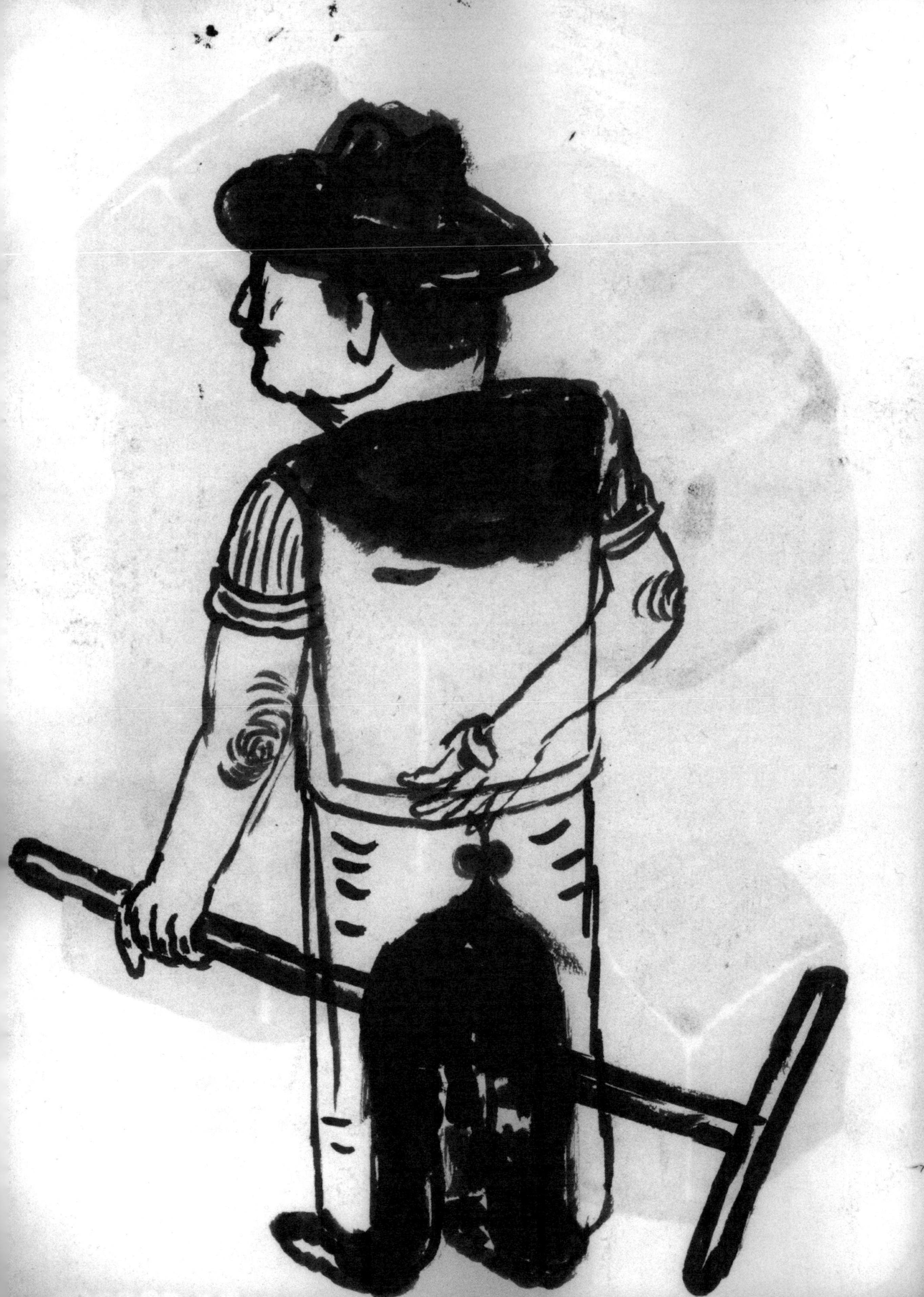

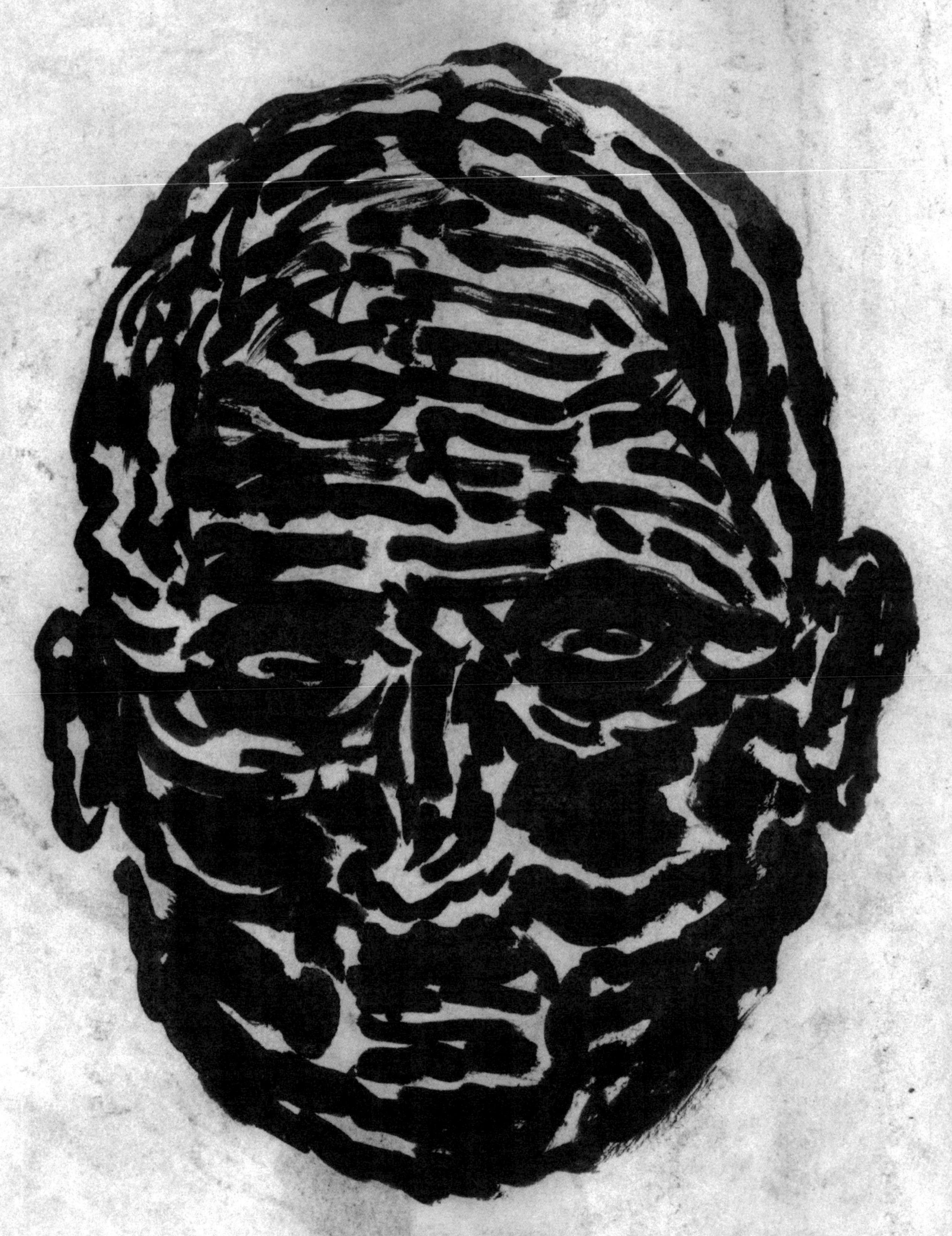

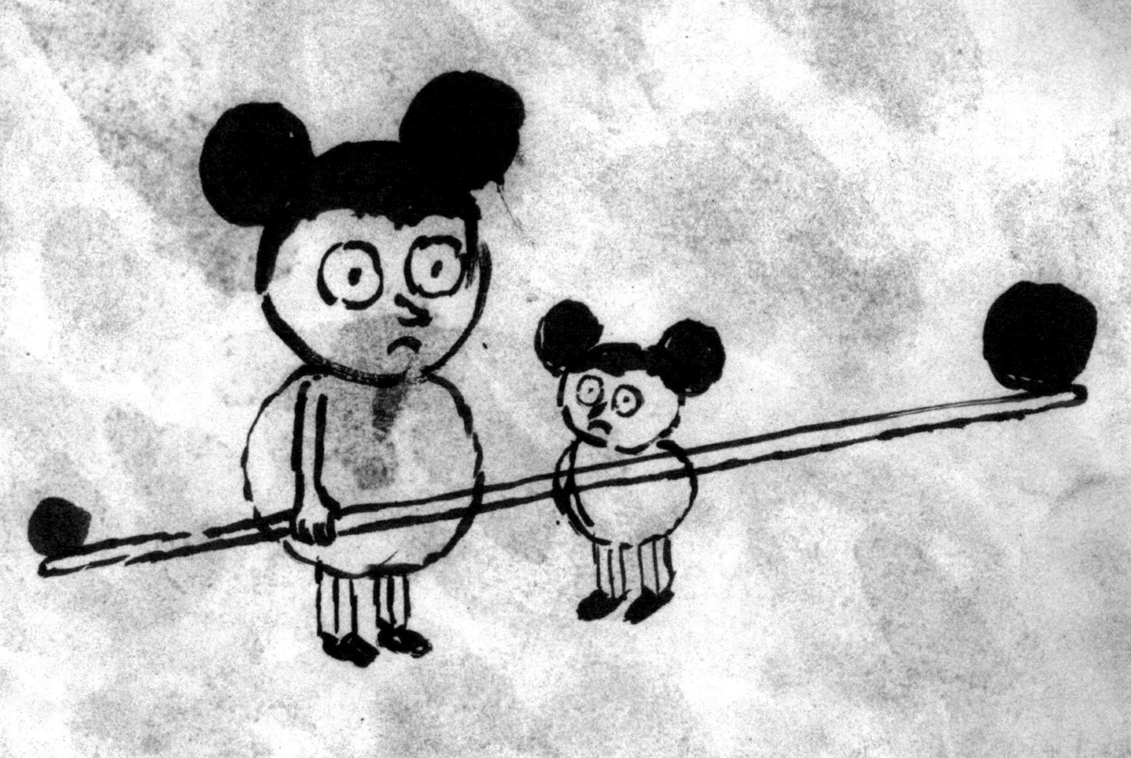

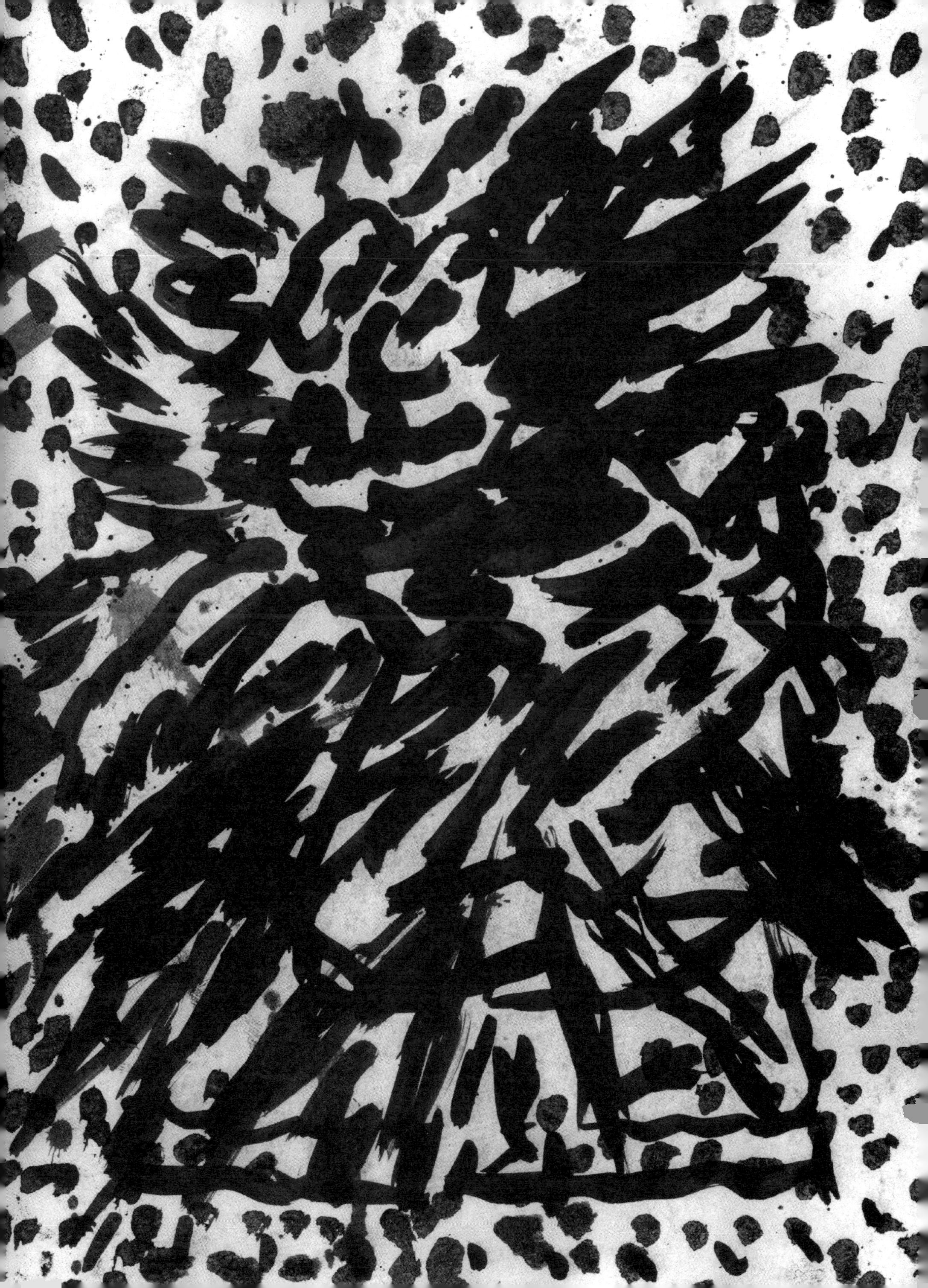

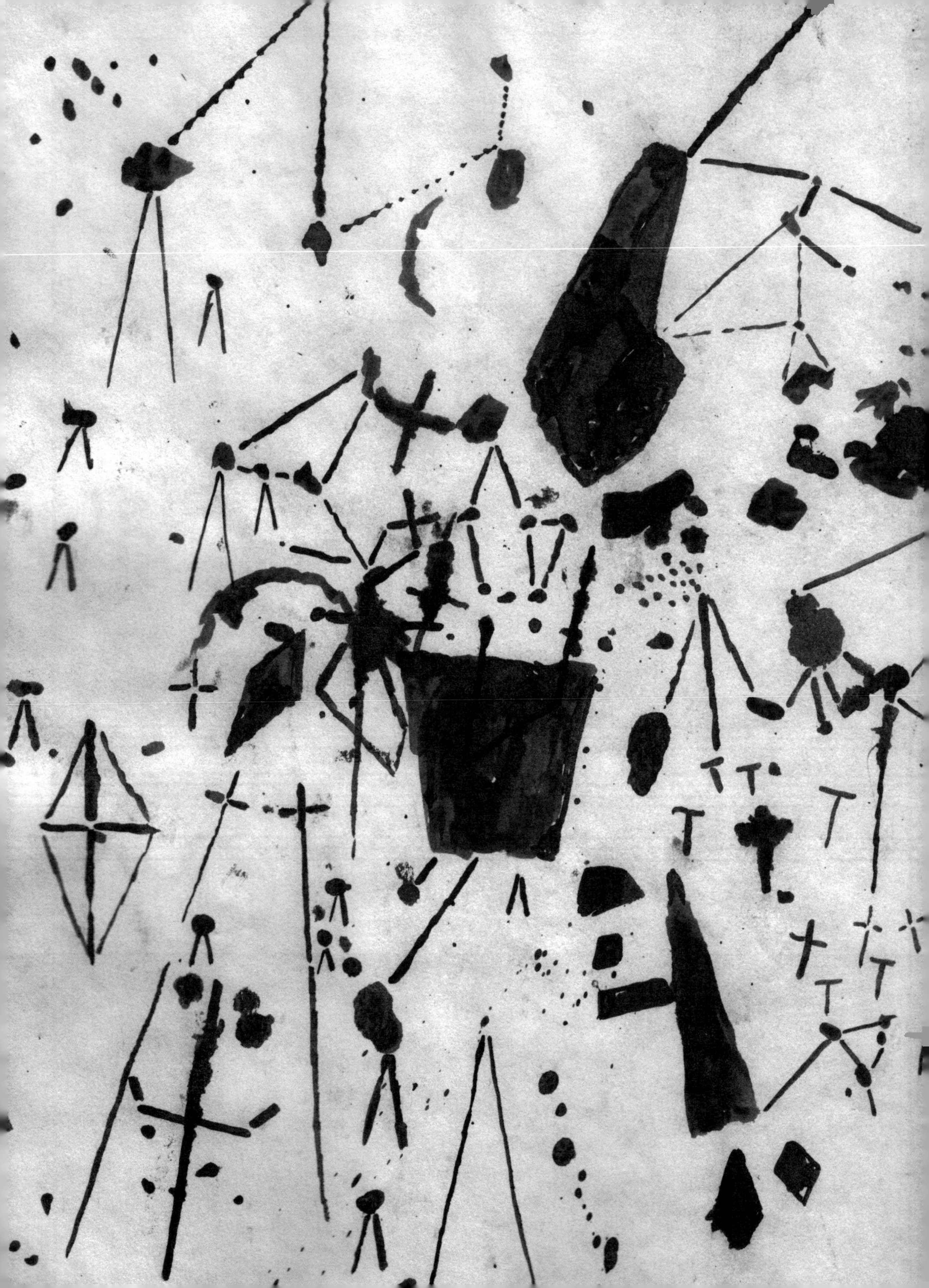

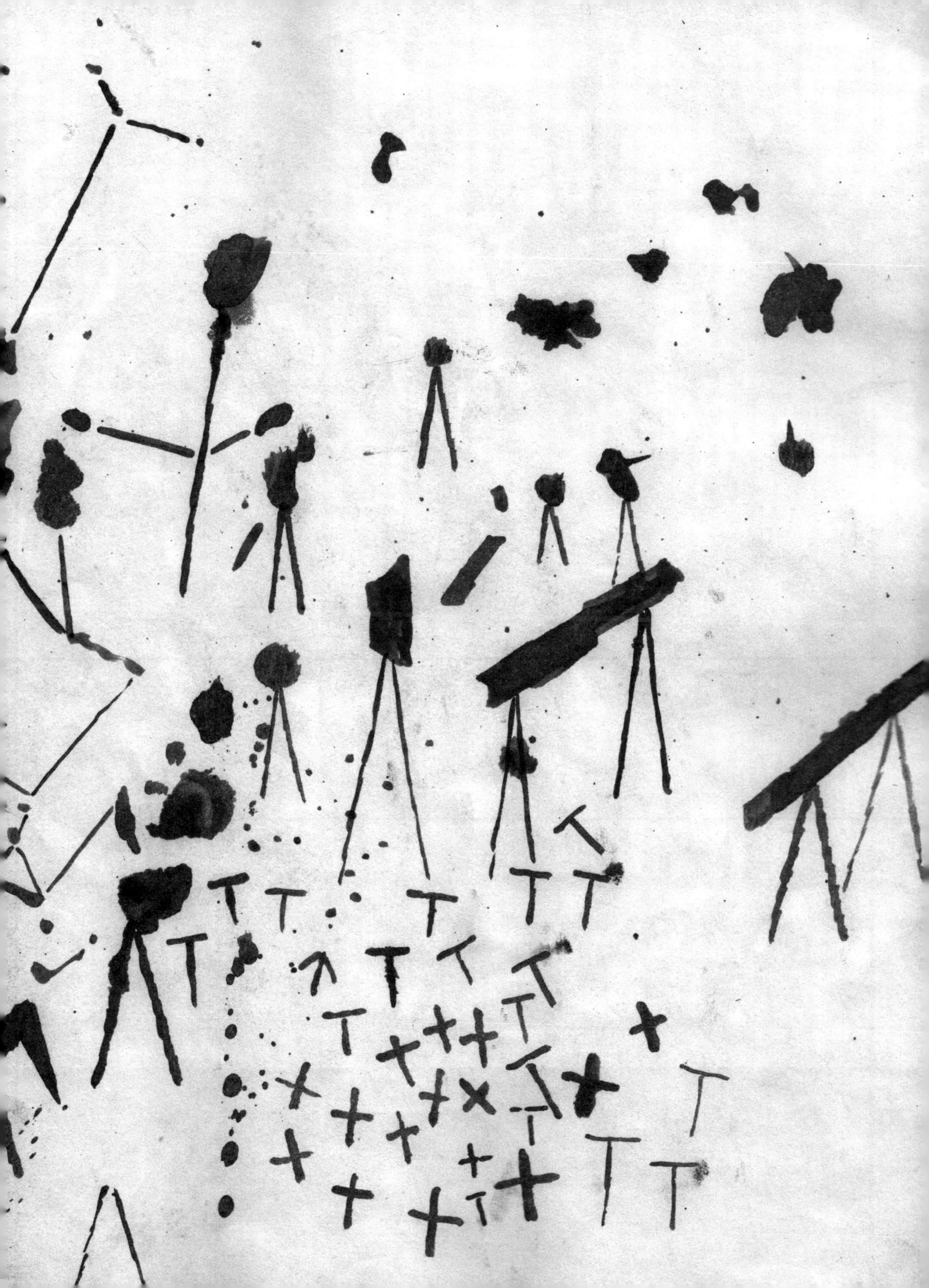

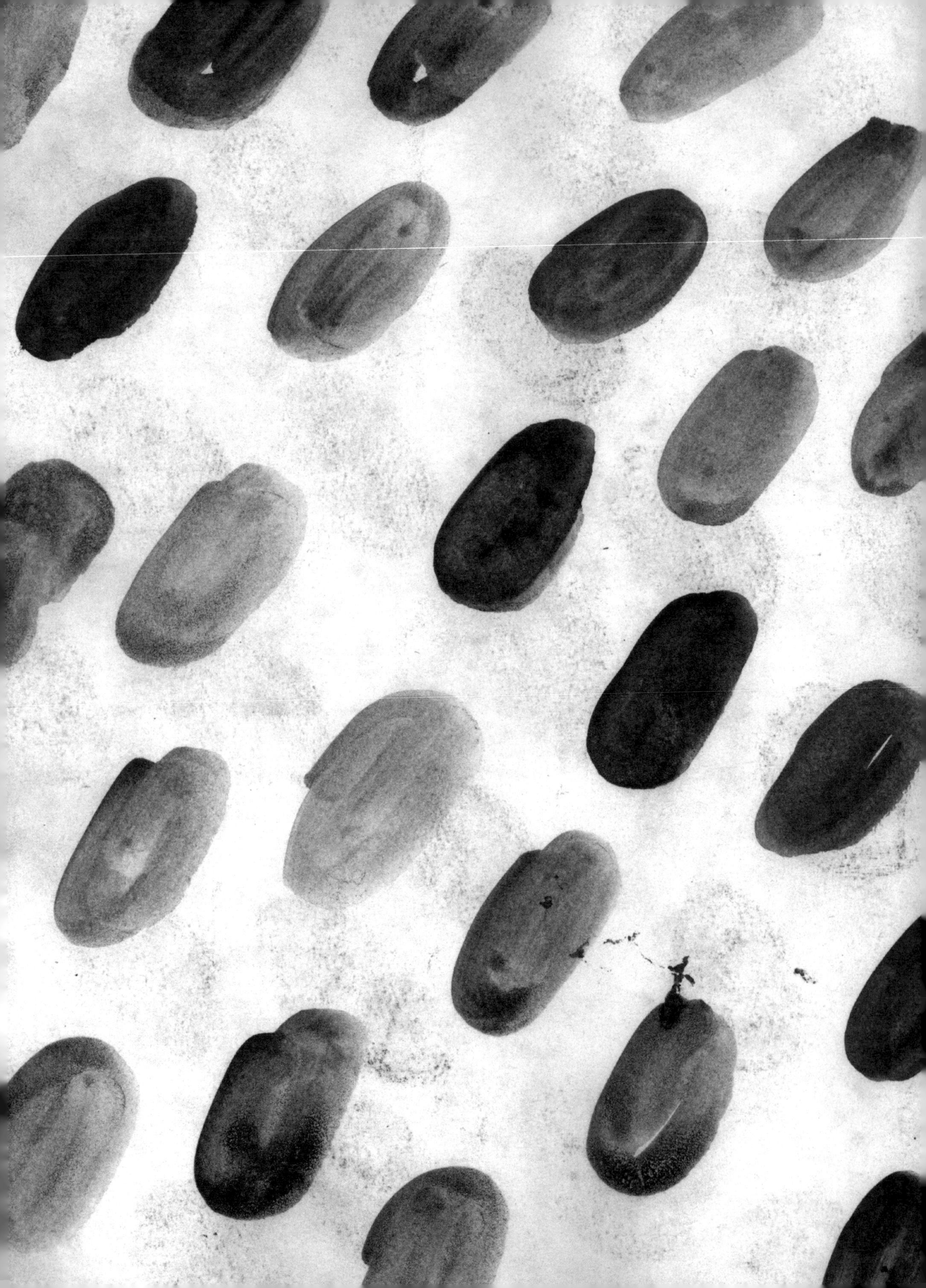

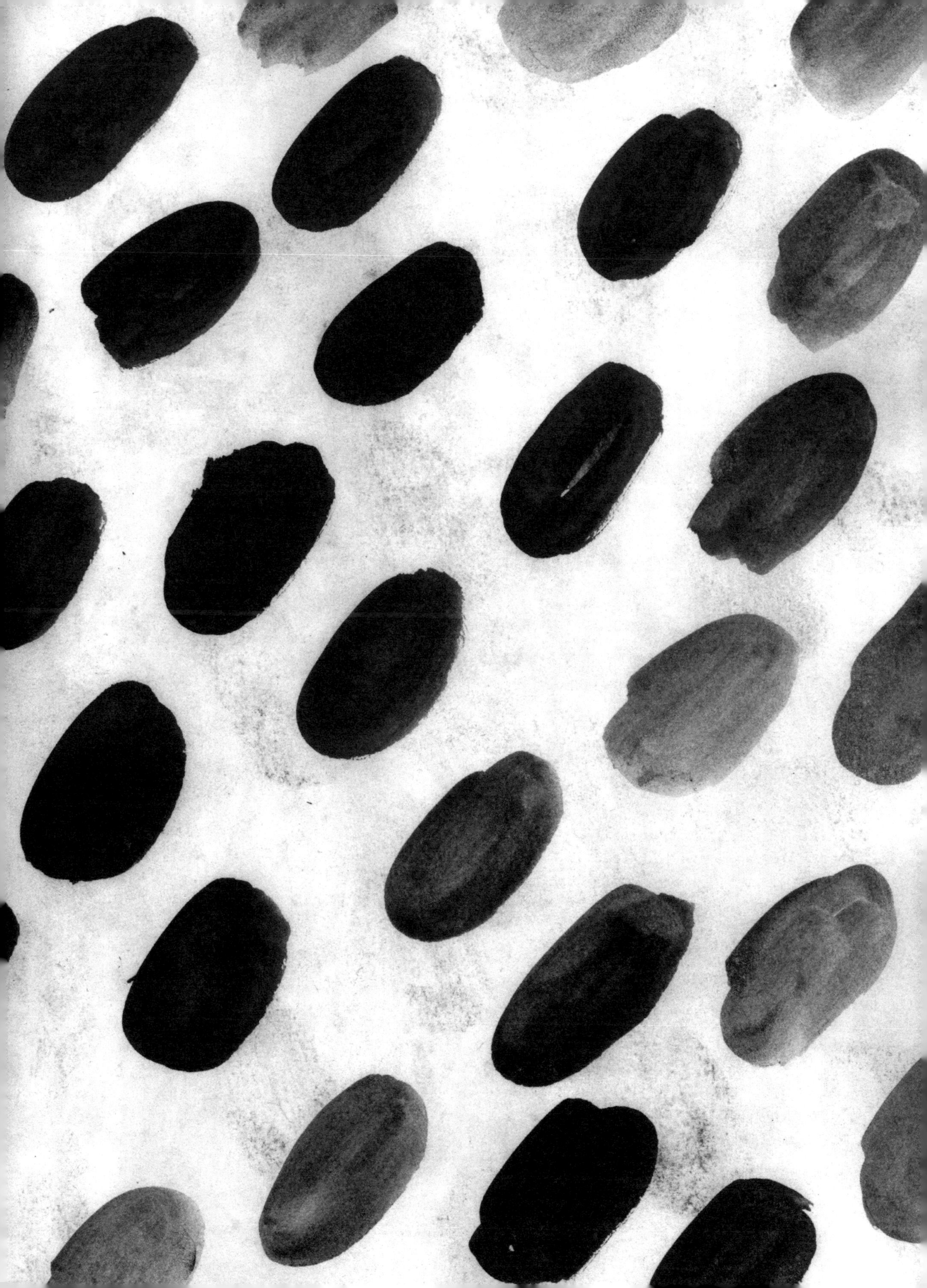

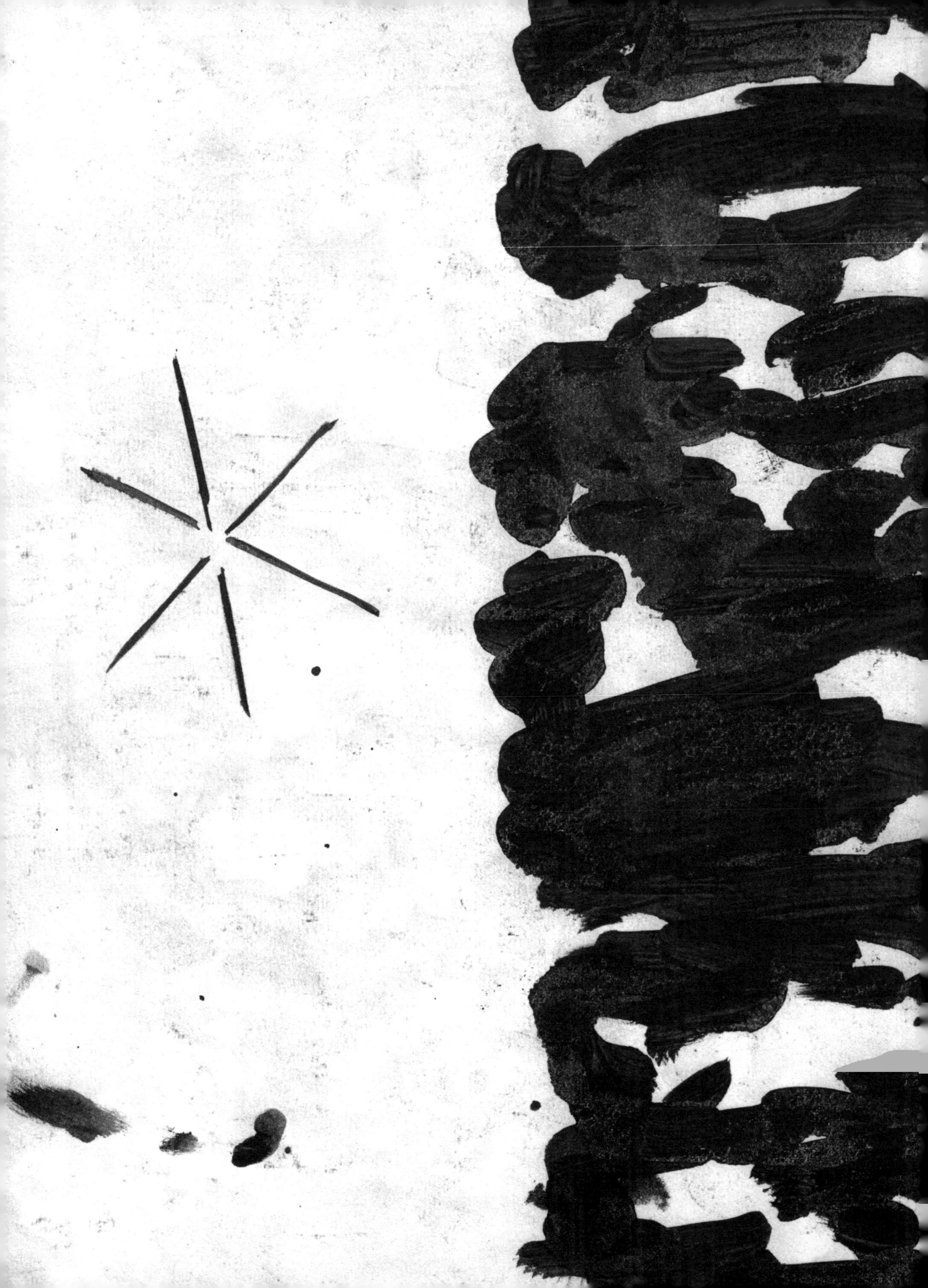

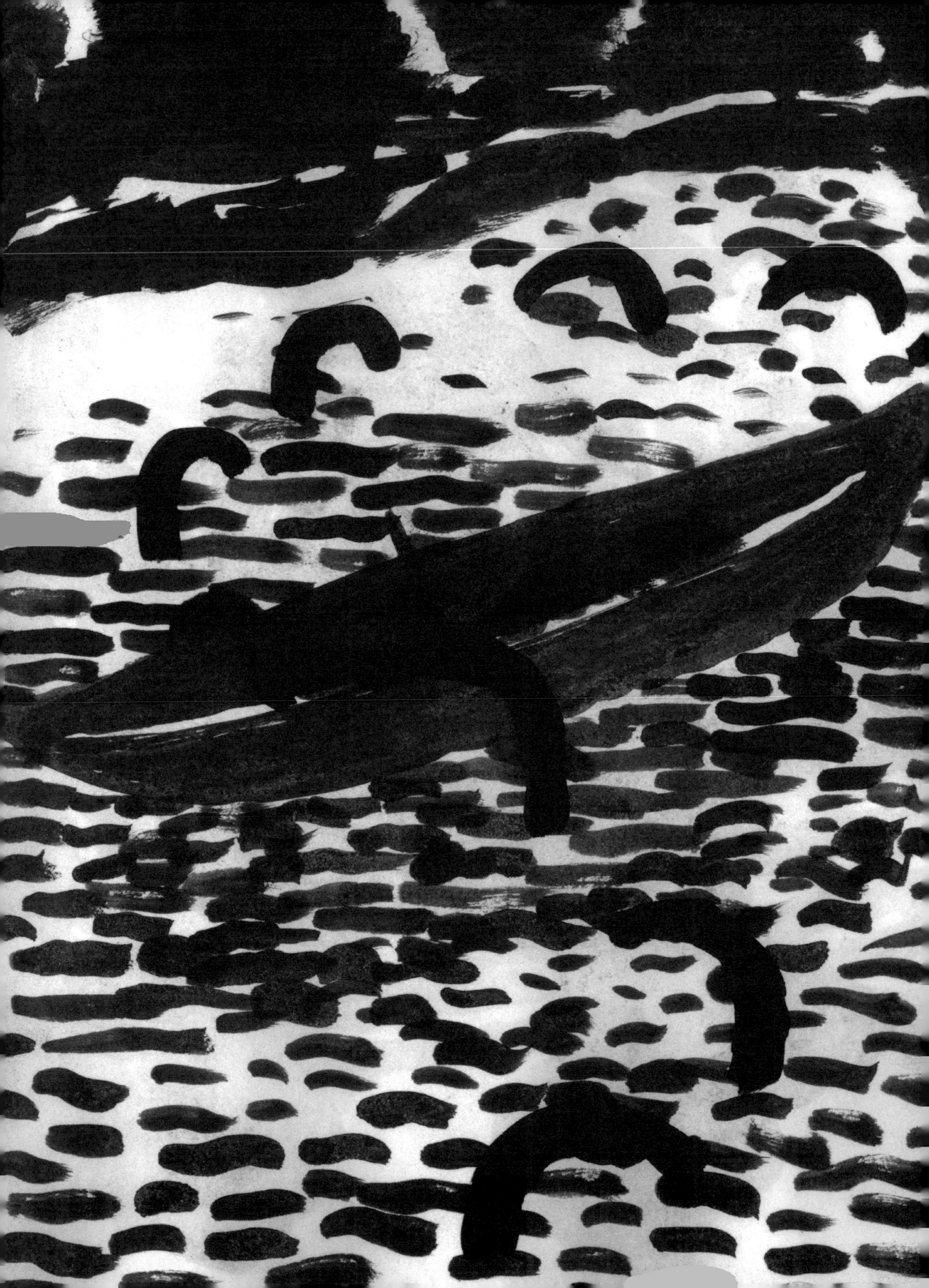

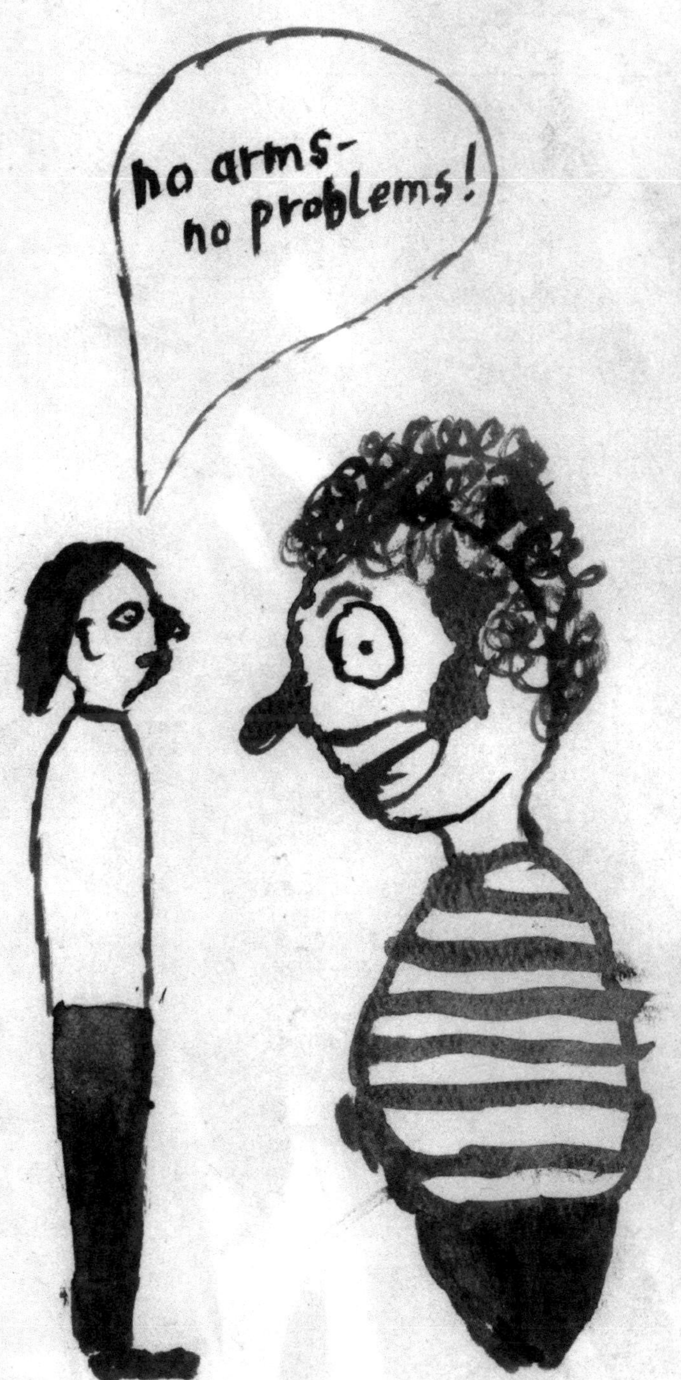
no arms-
no problems!

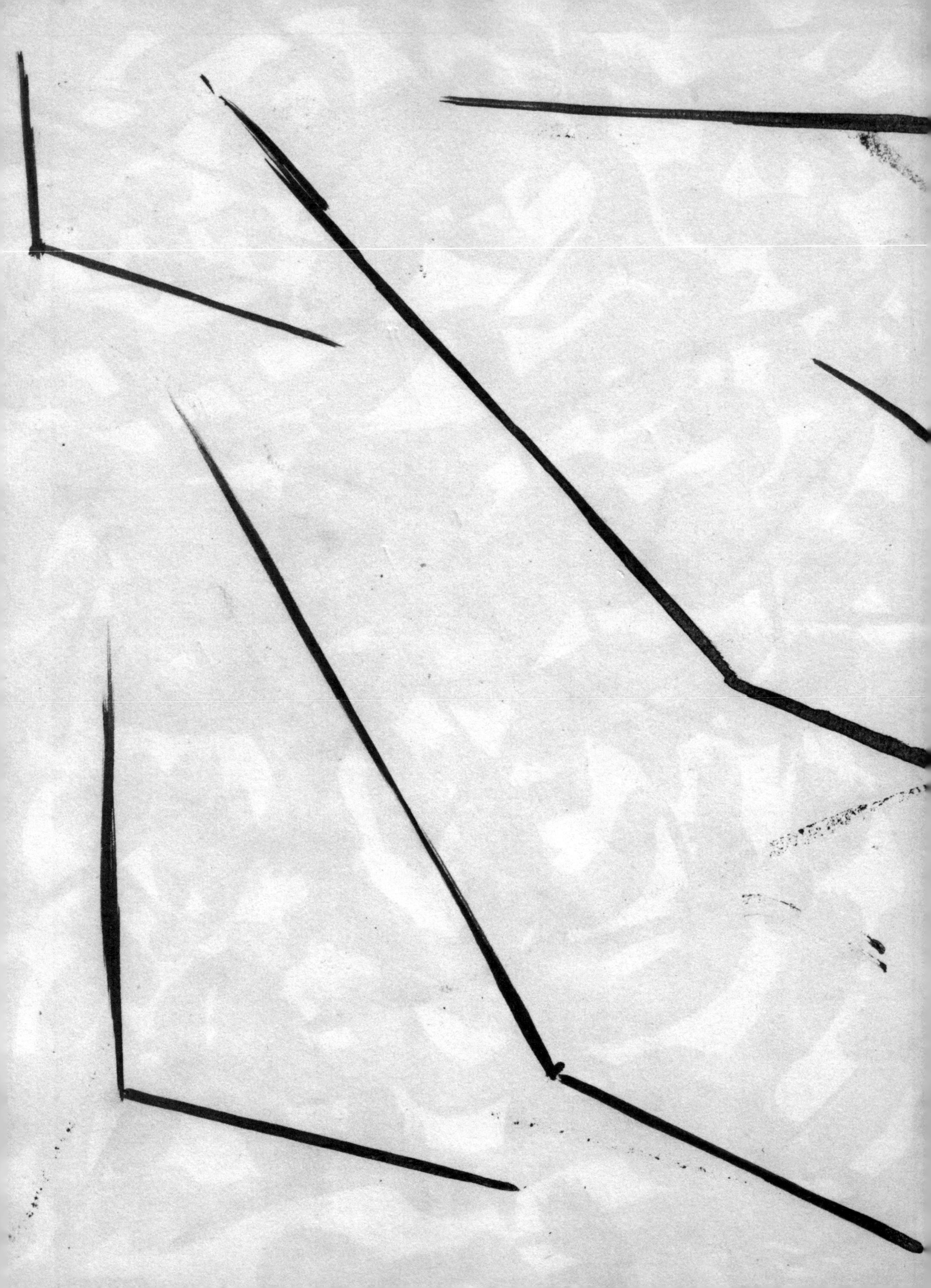

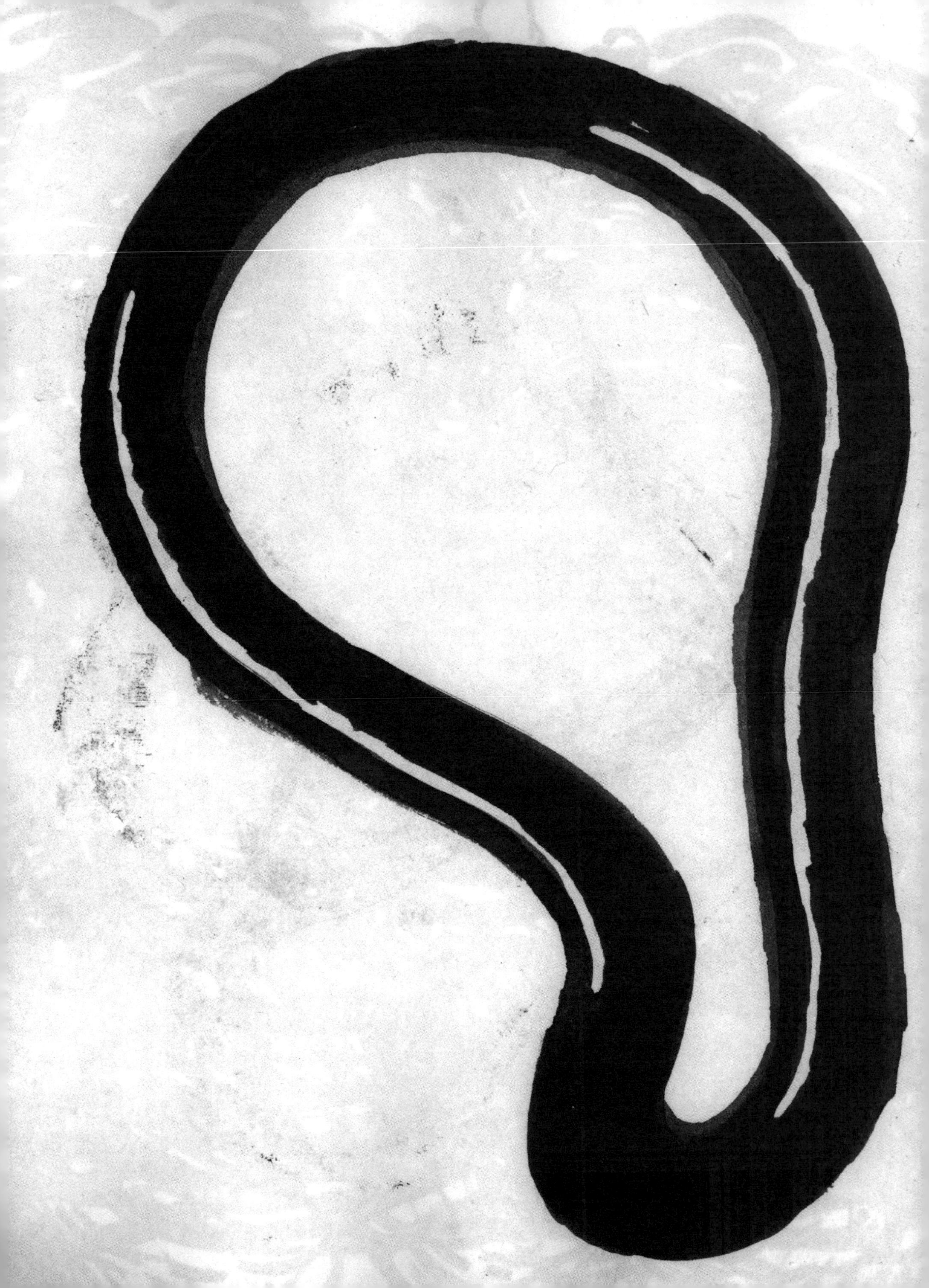

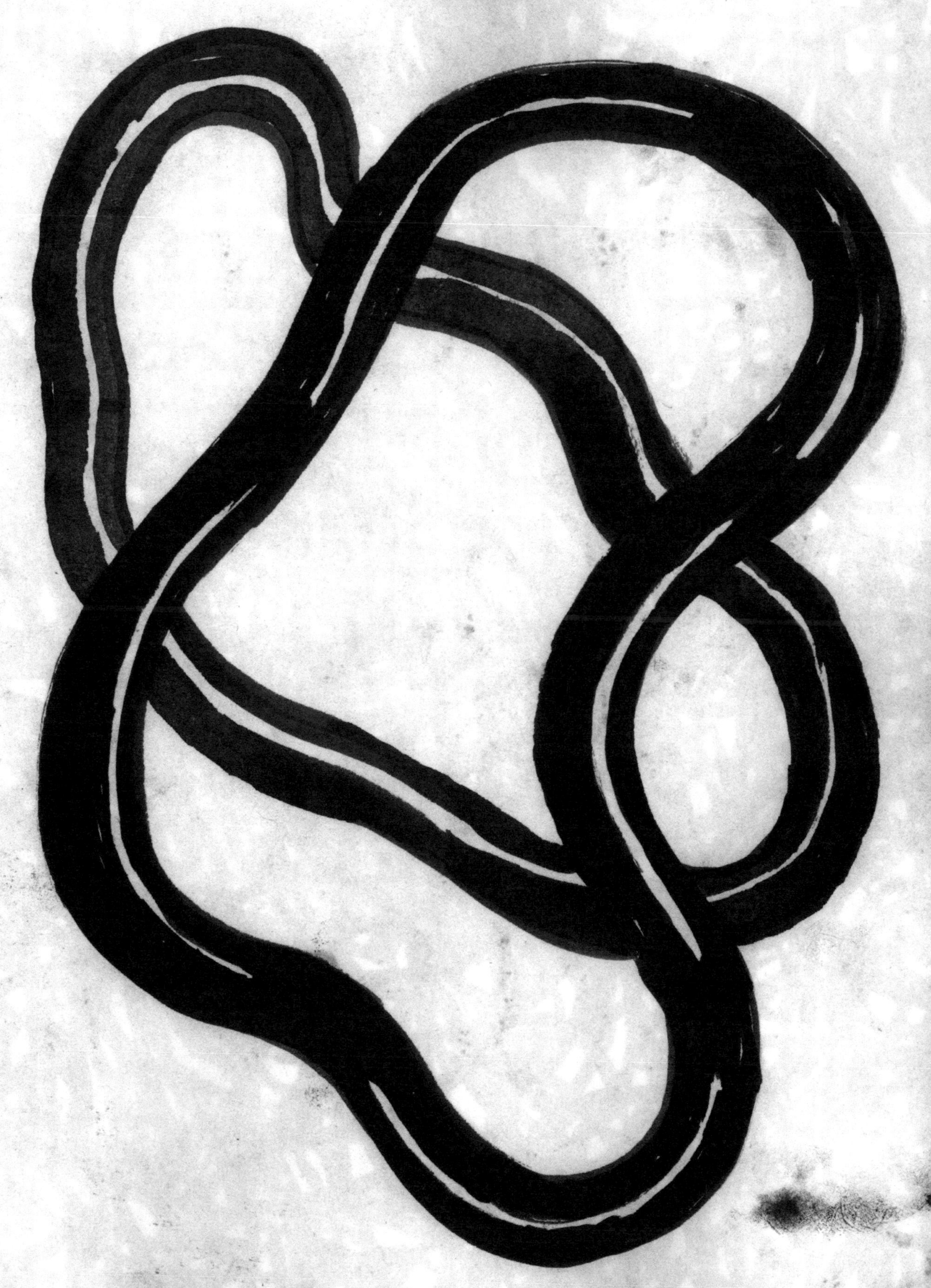

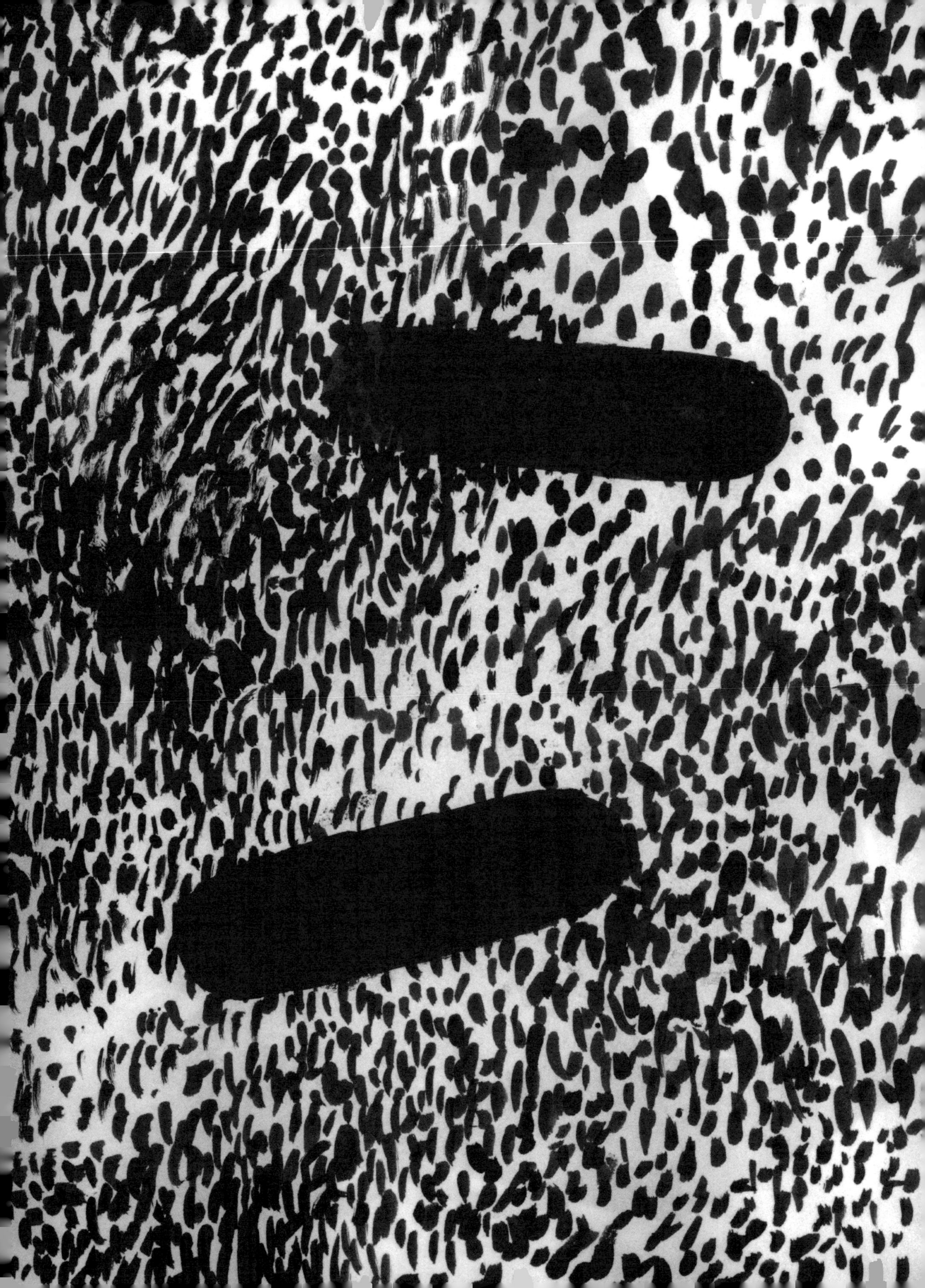

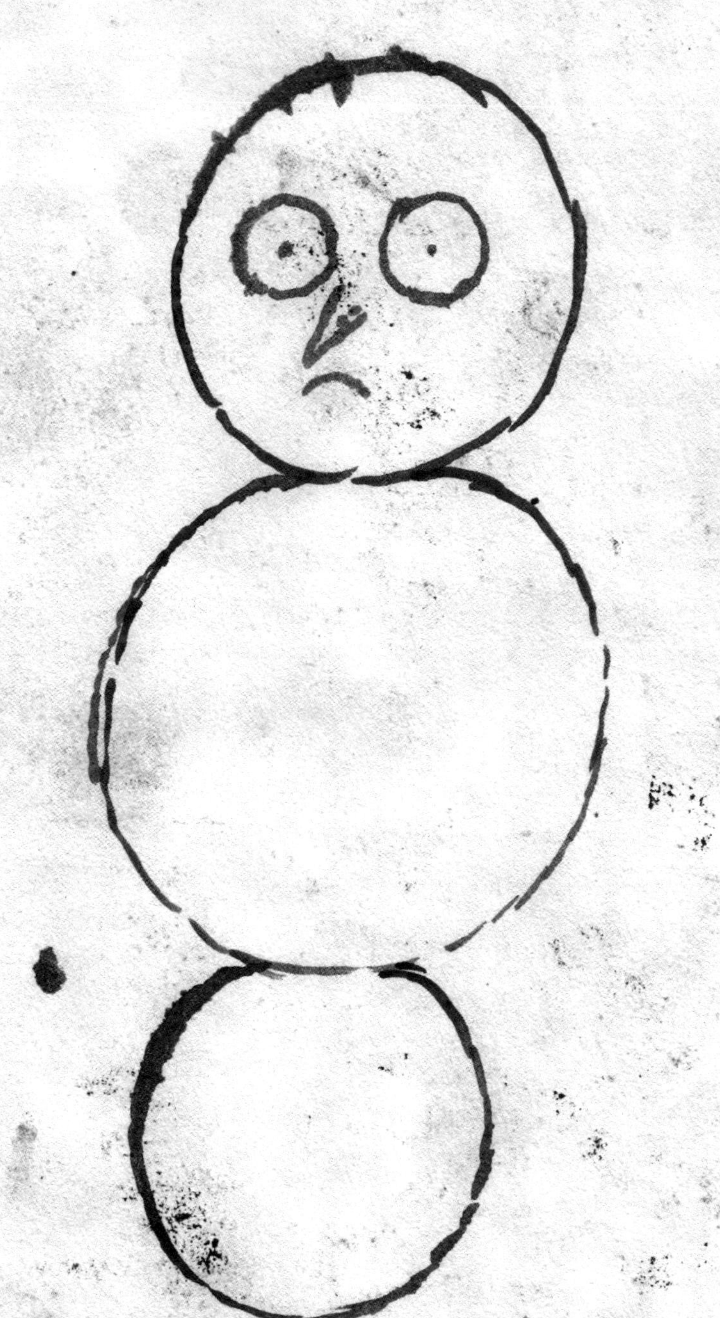

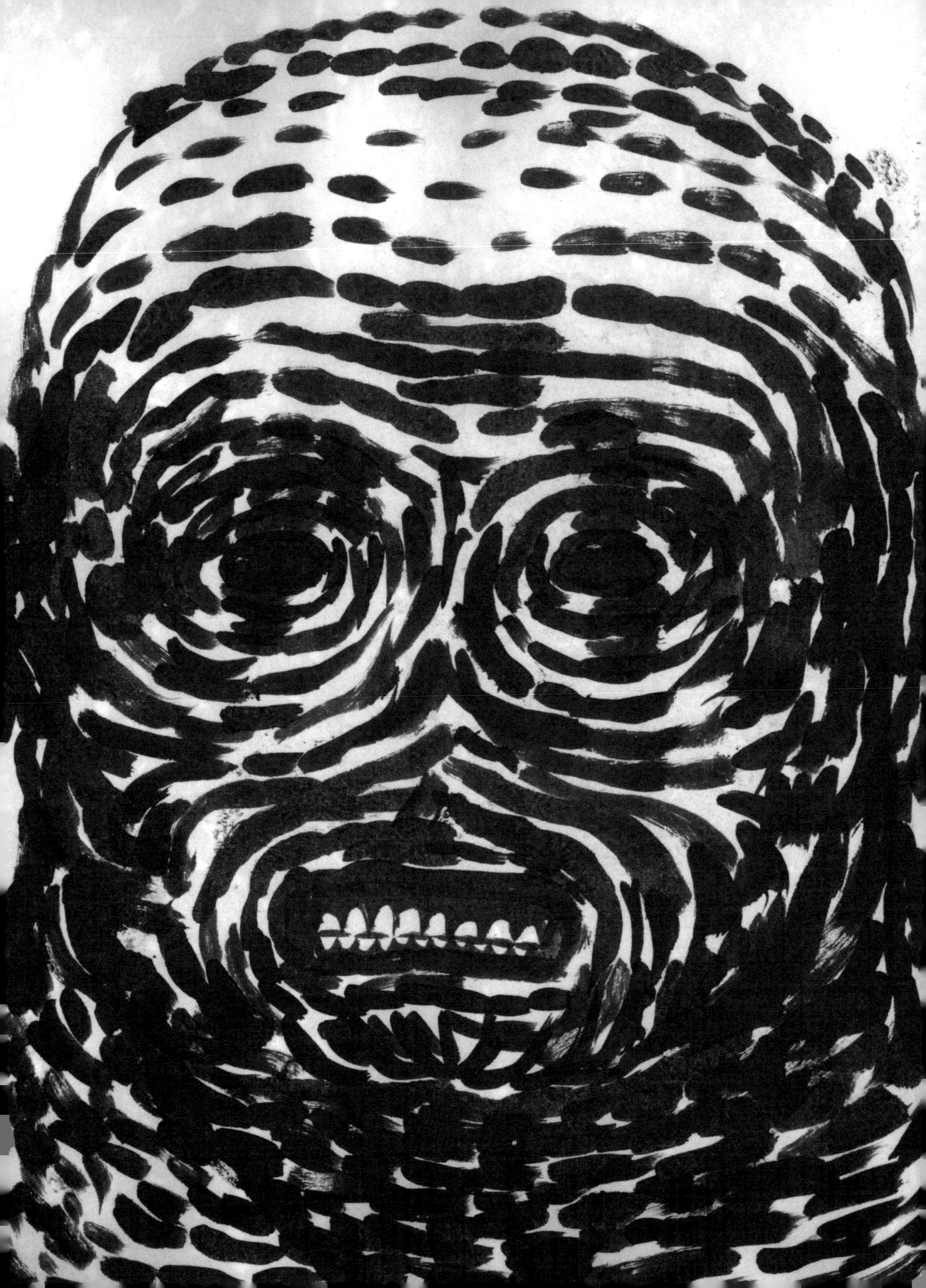

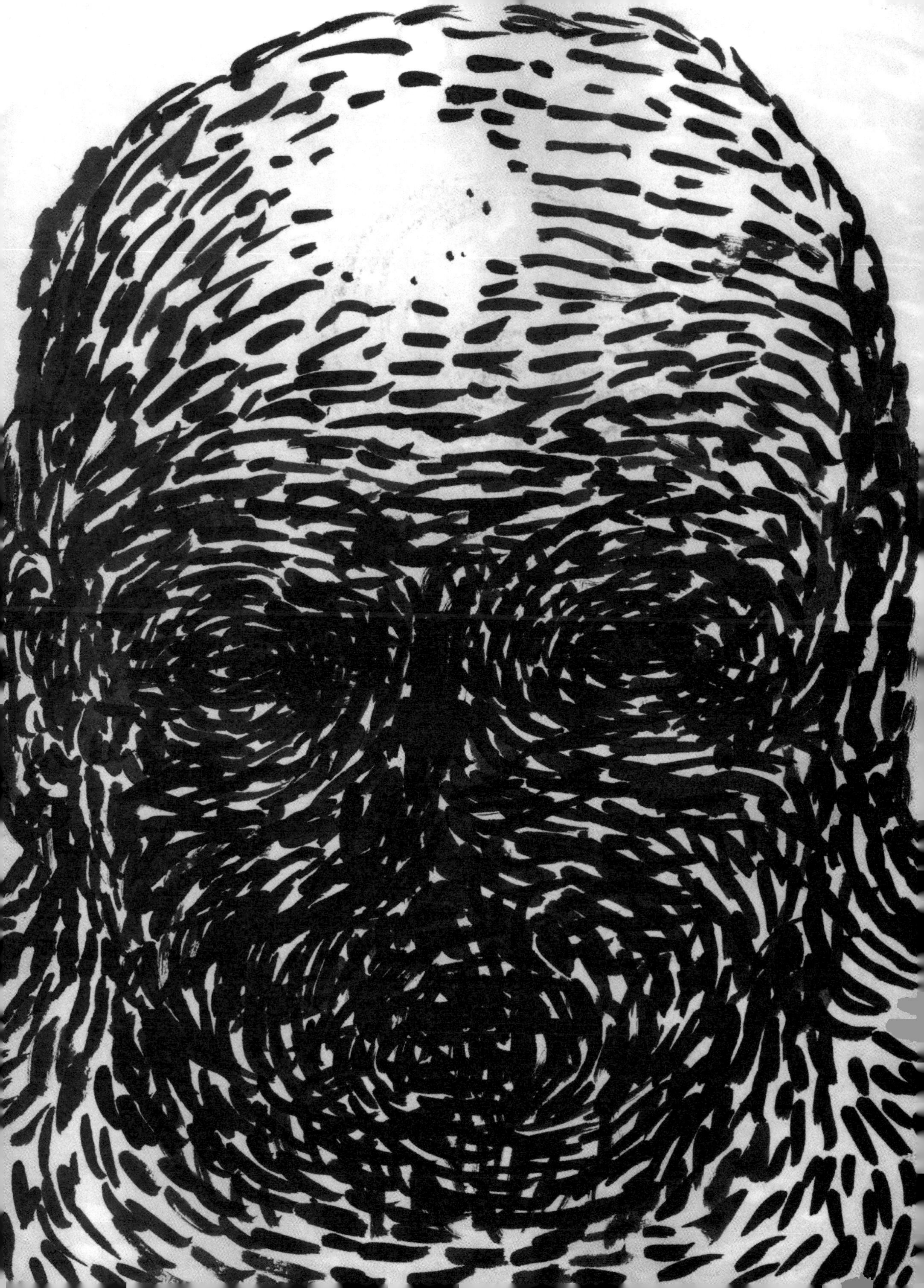

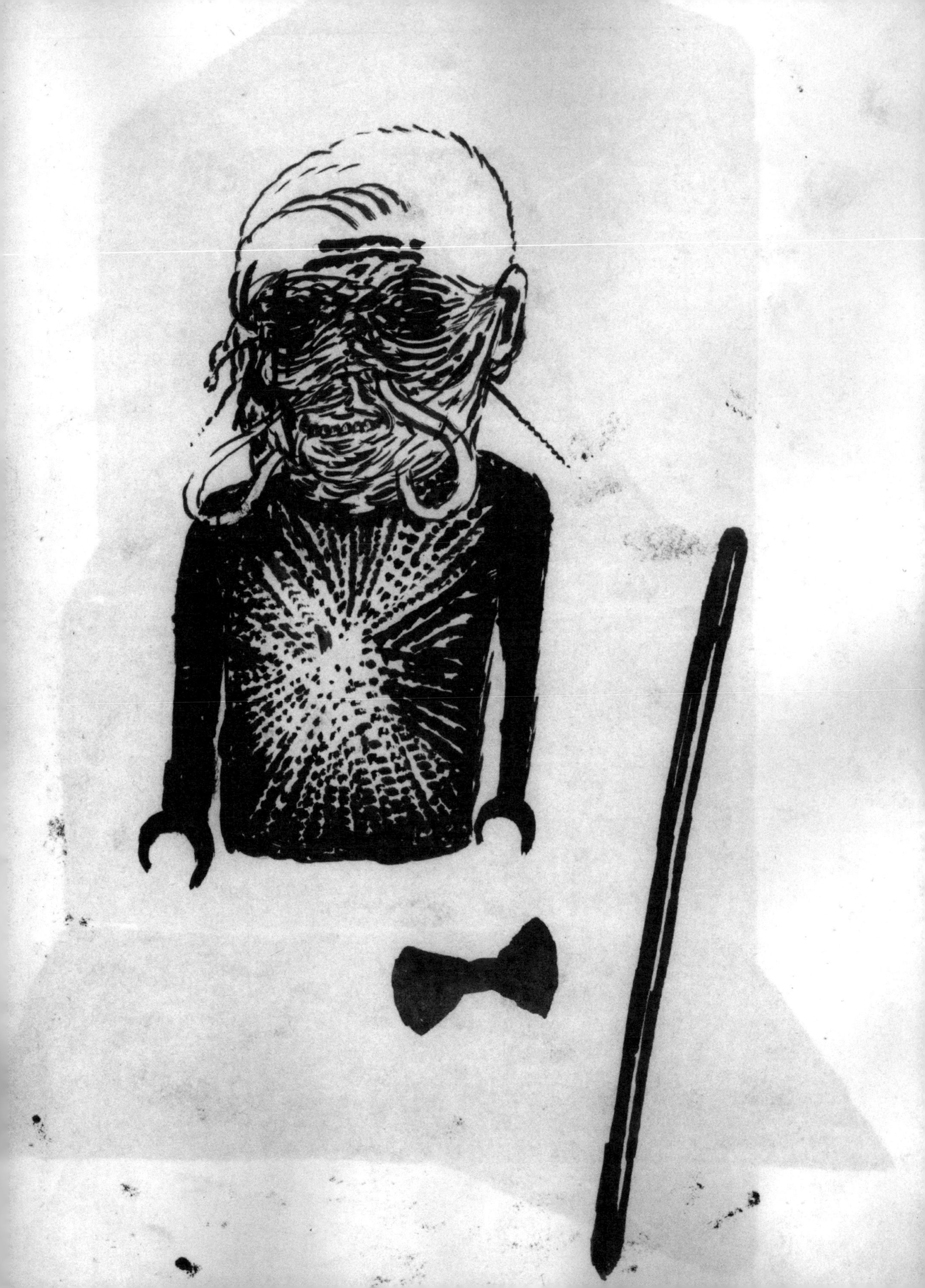

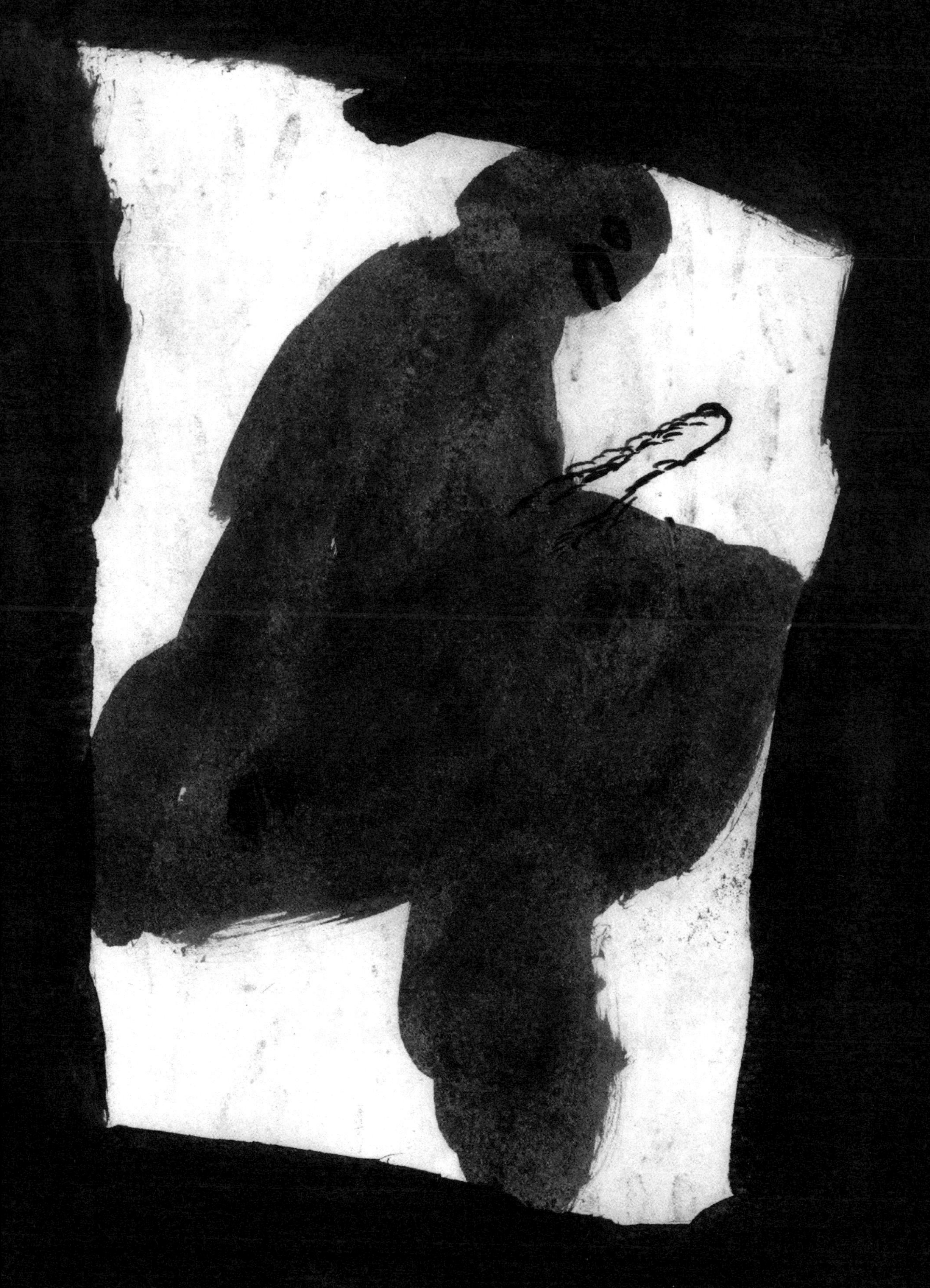

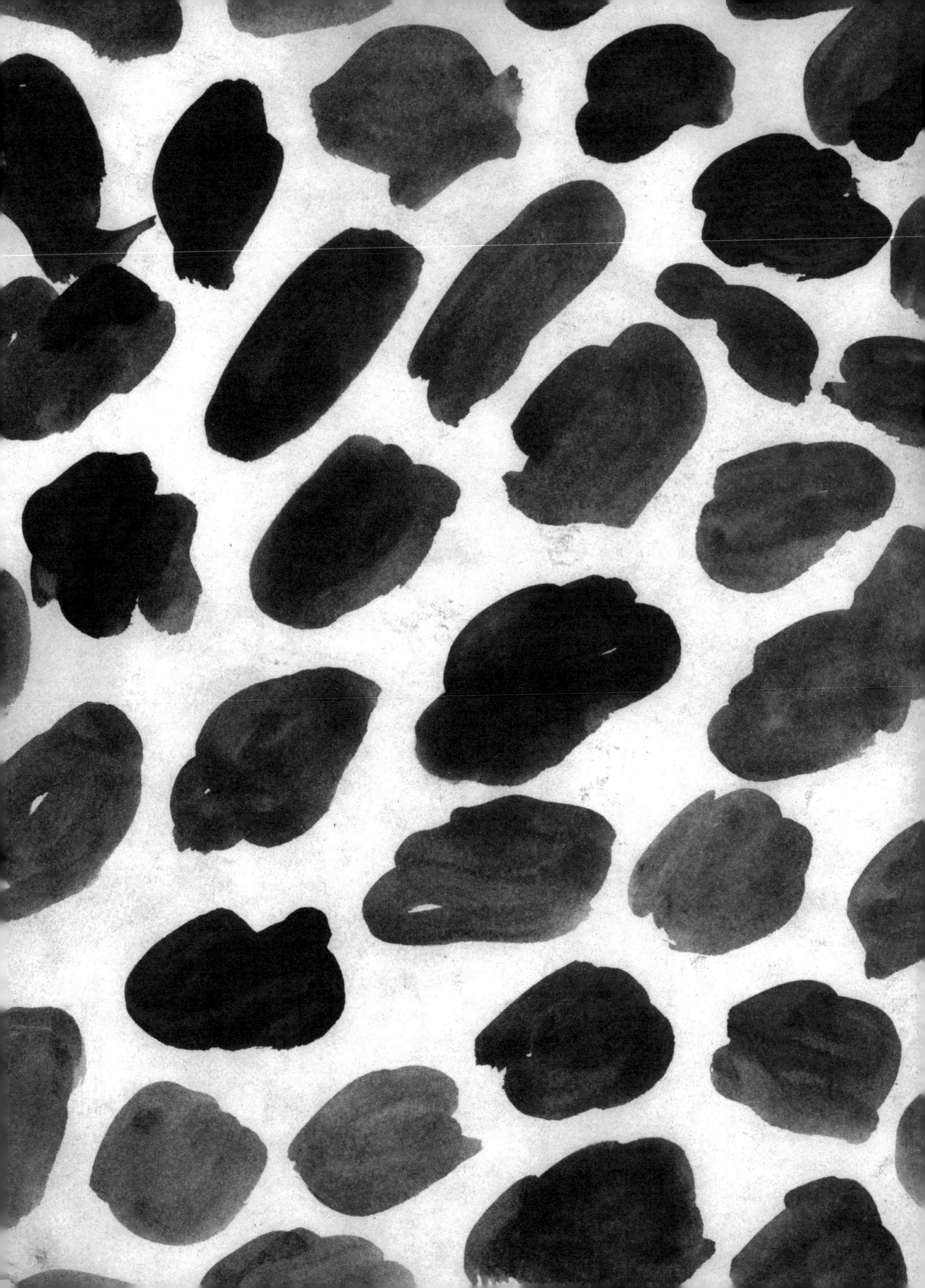

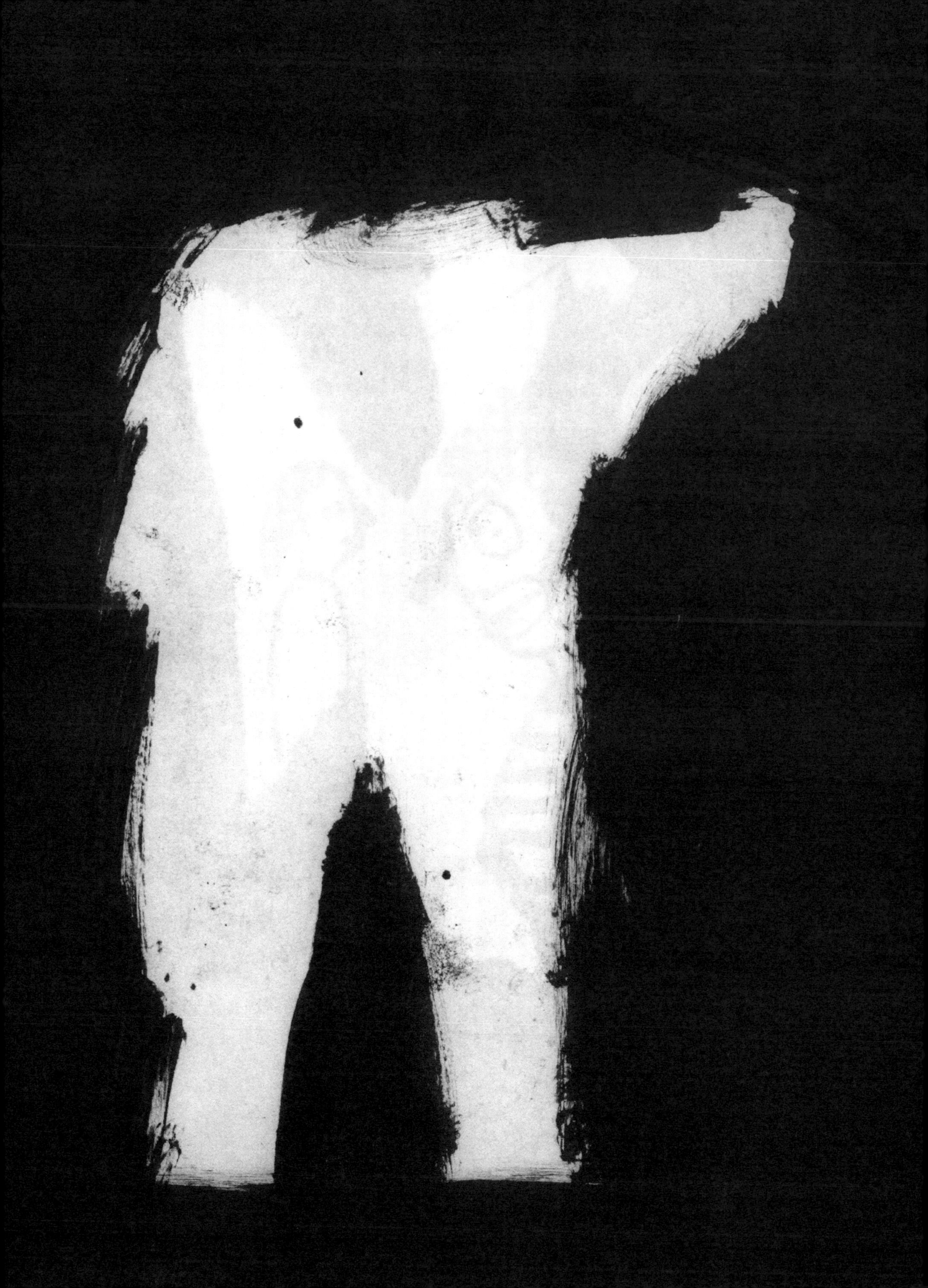

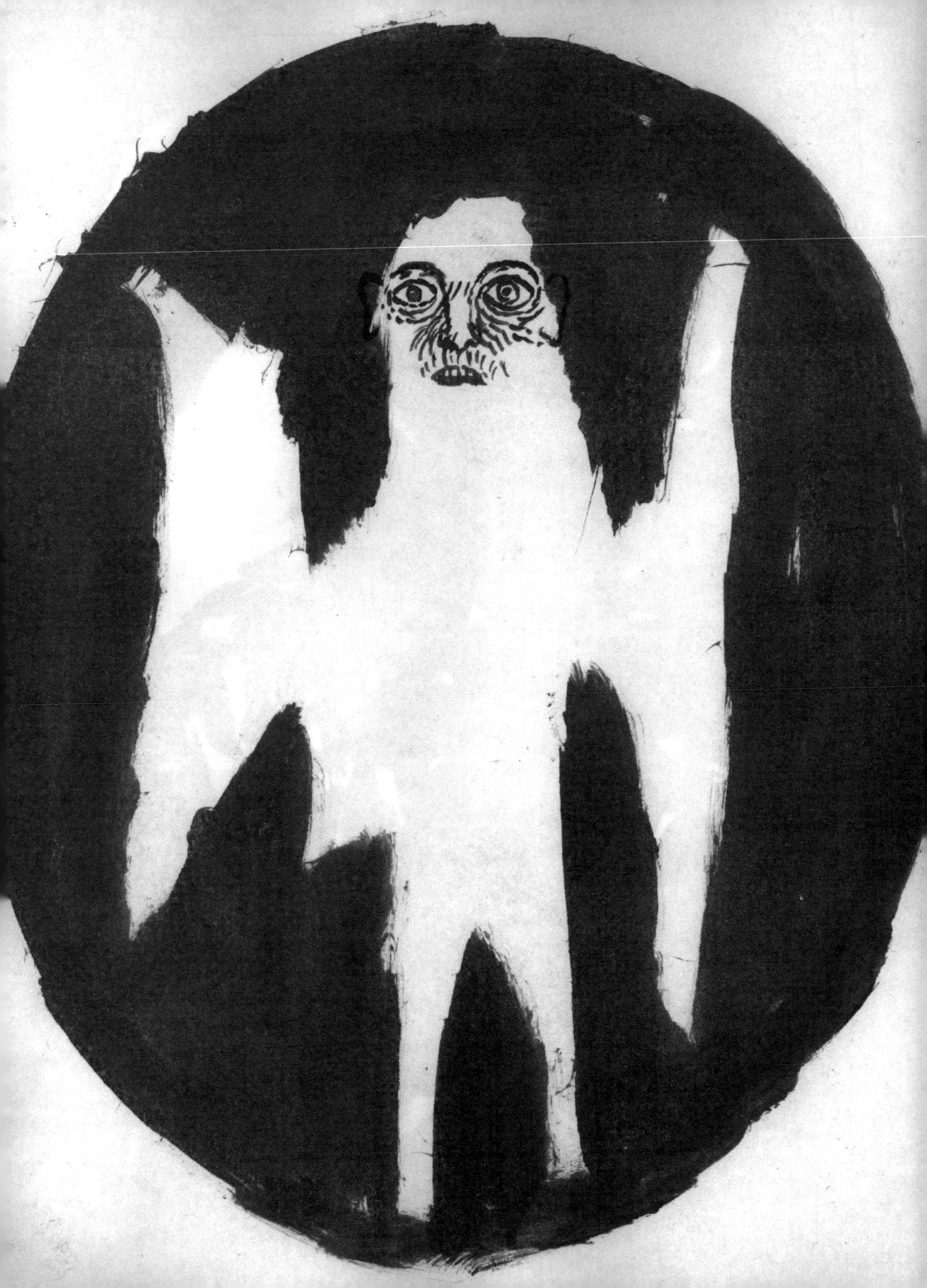

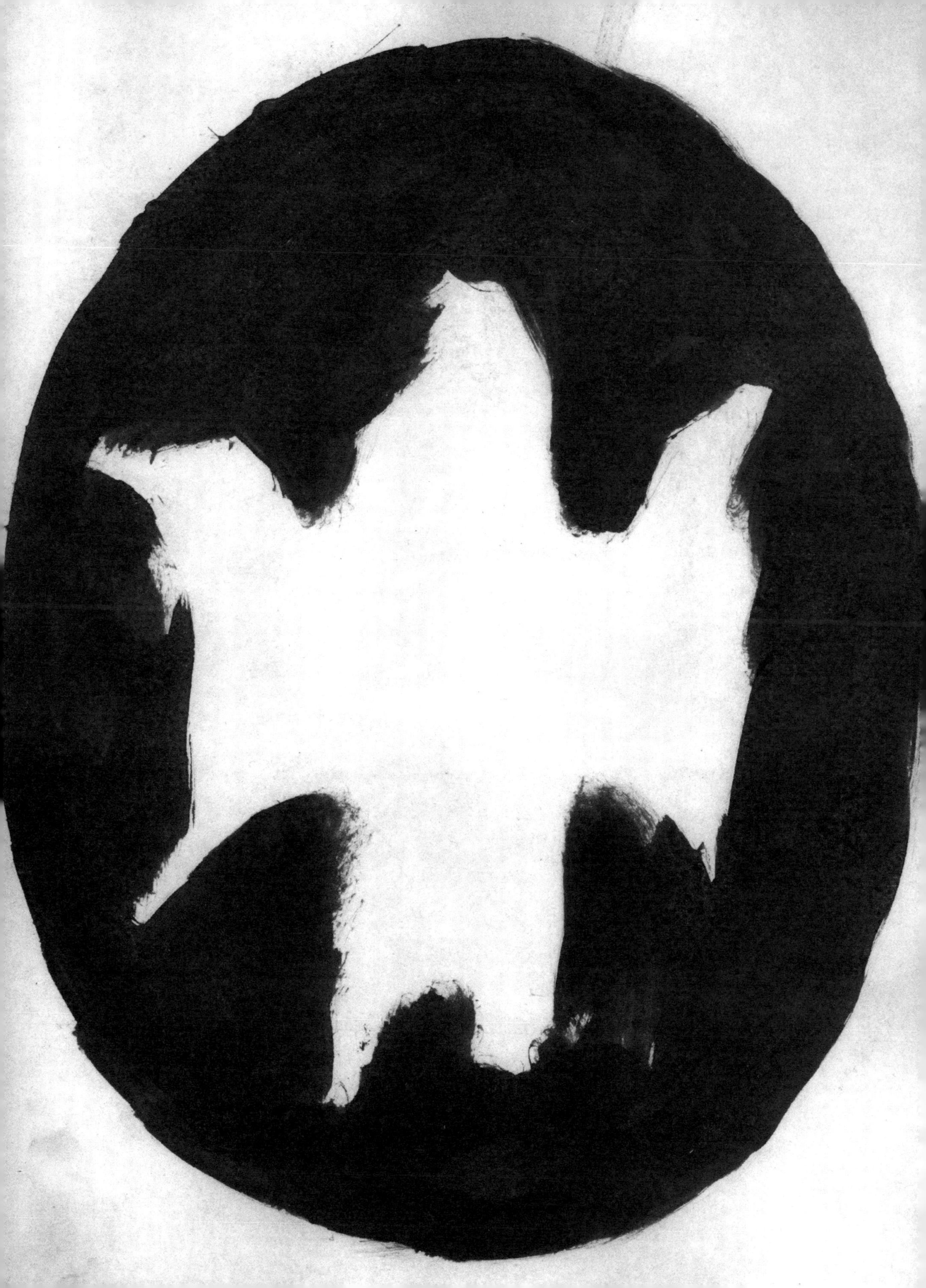

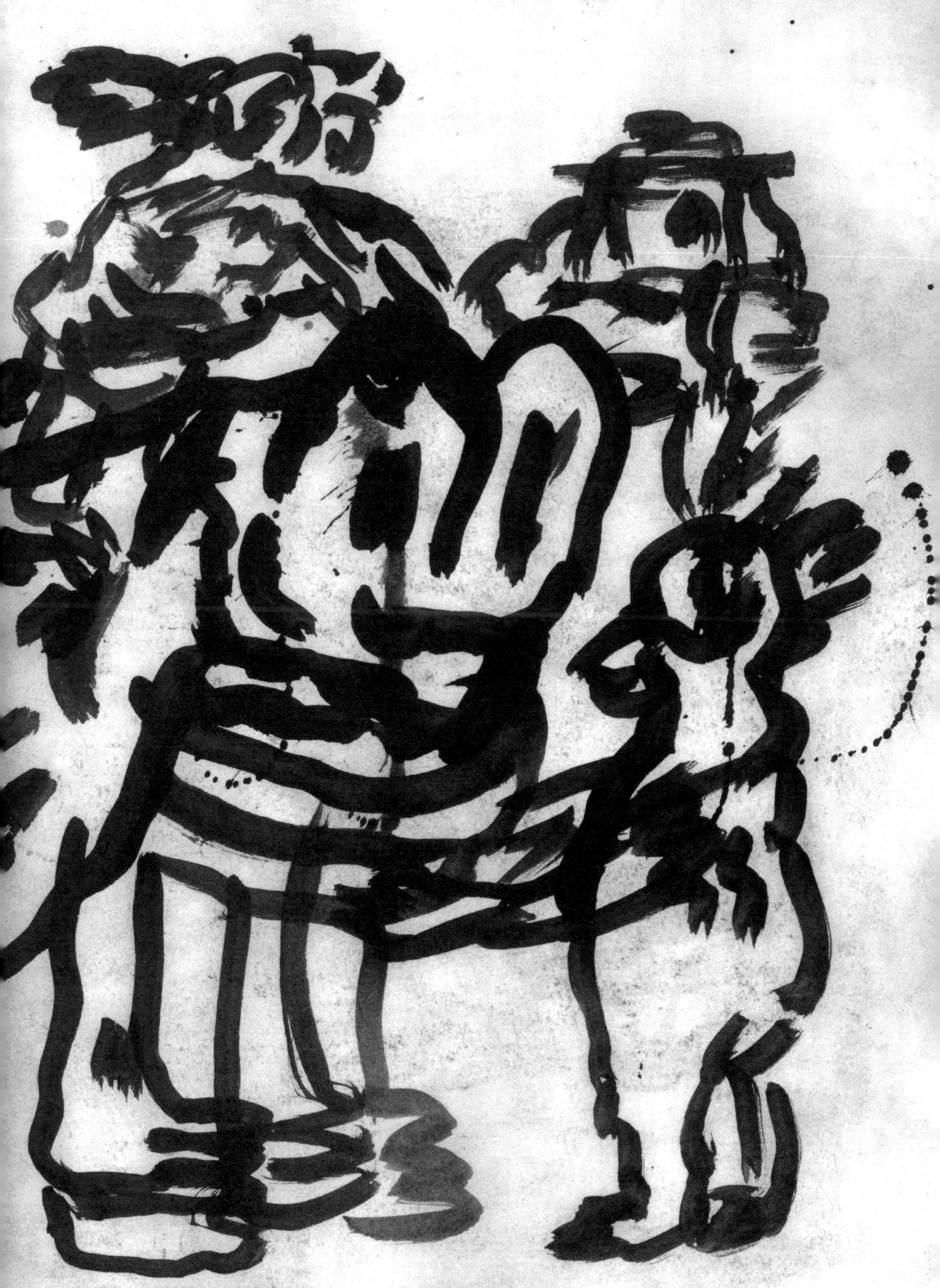

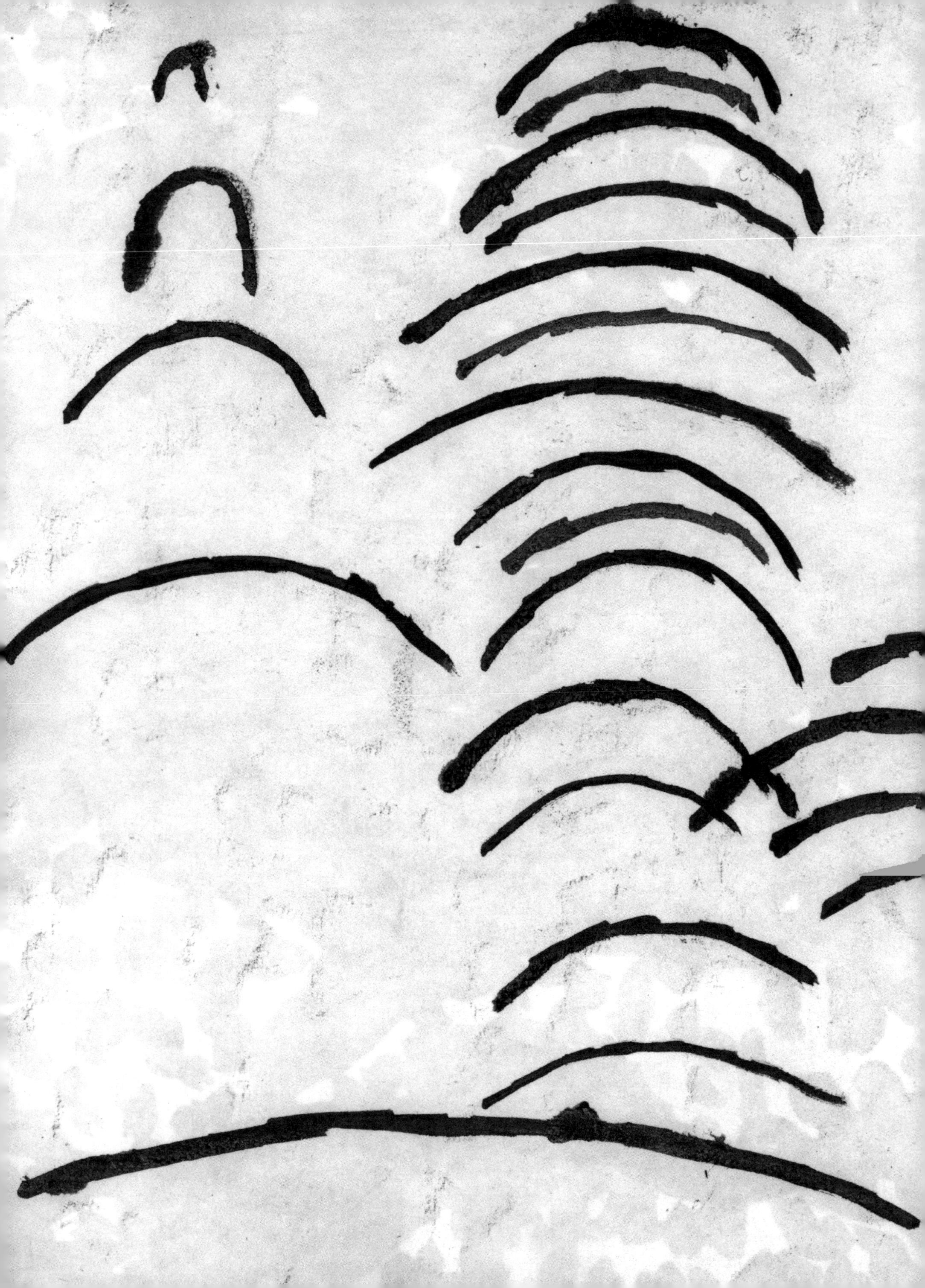

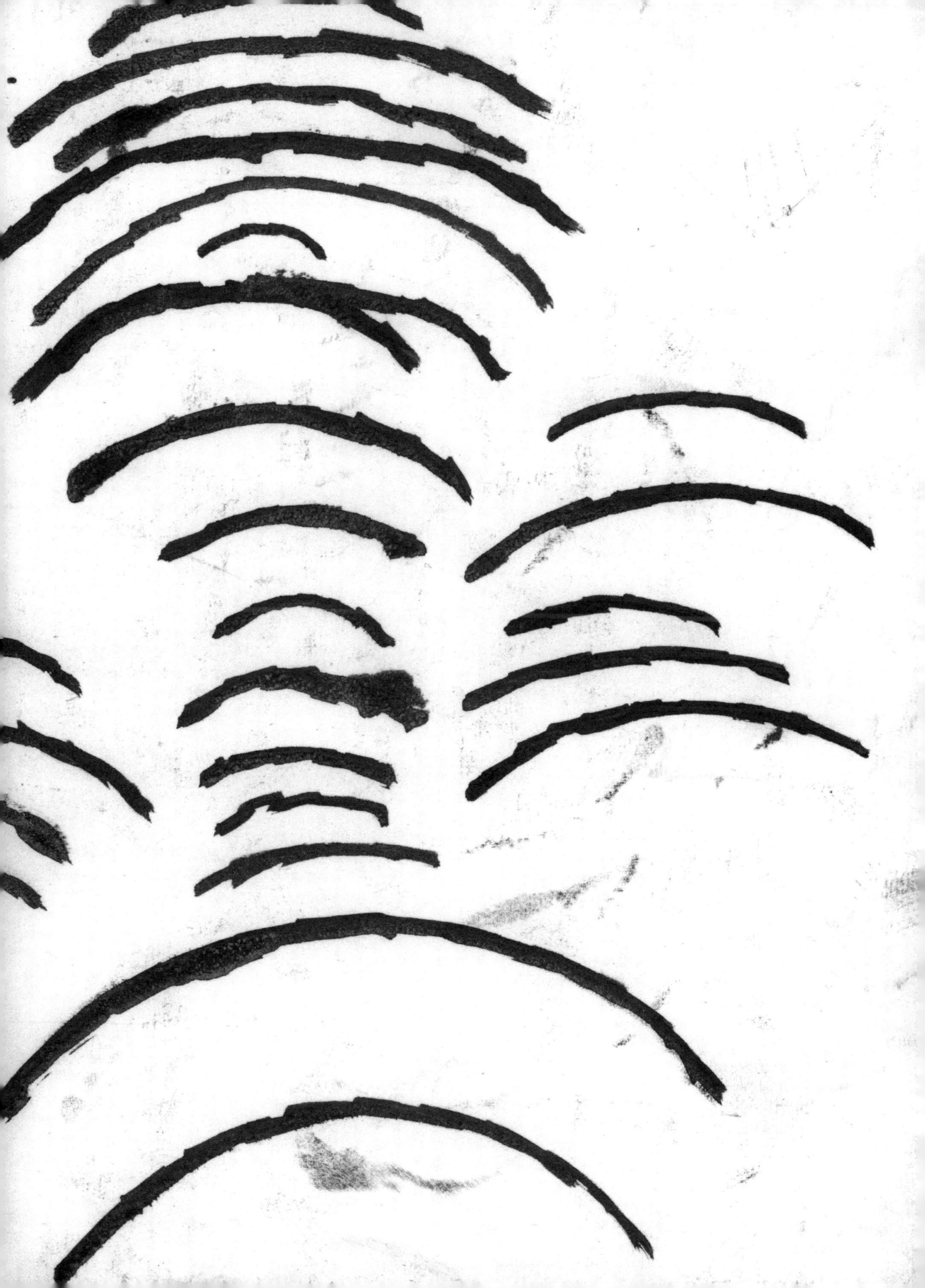

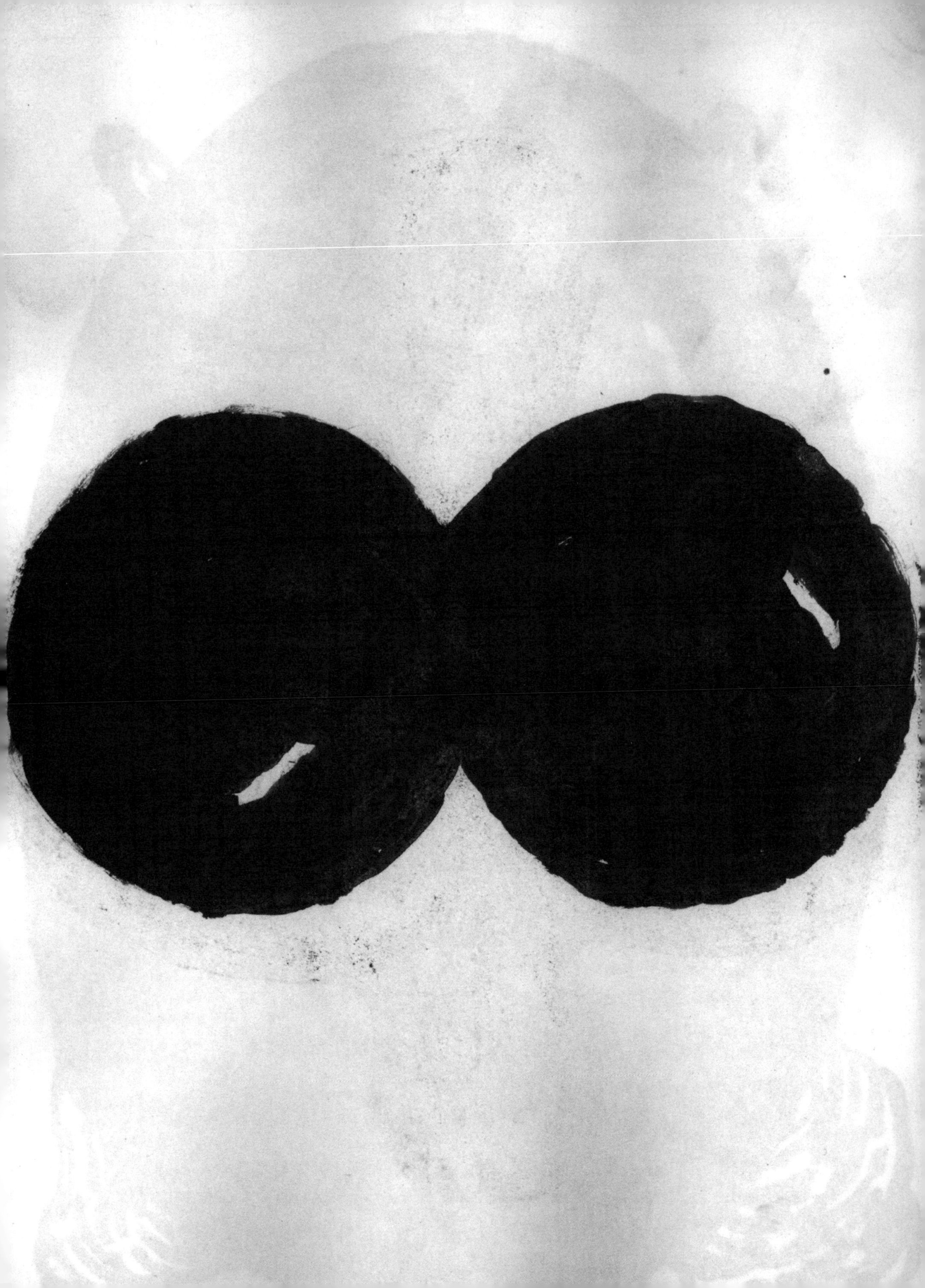

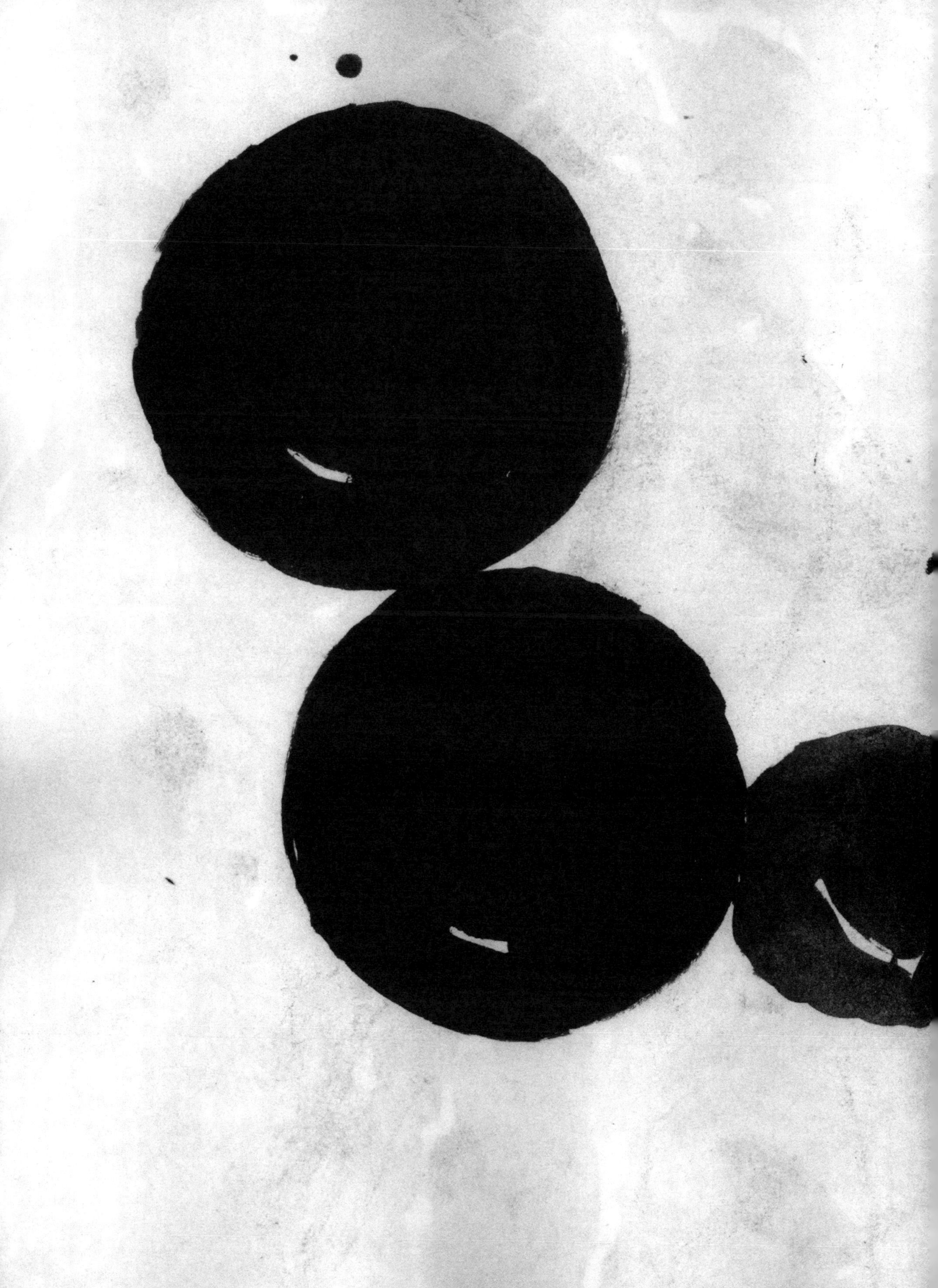

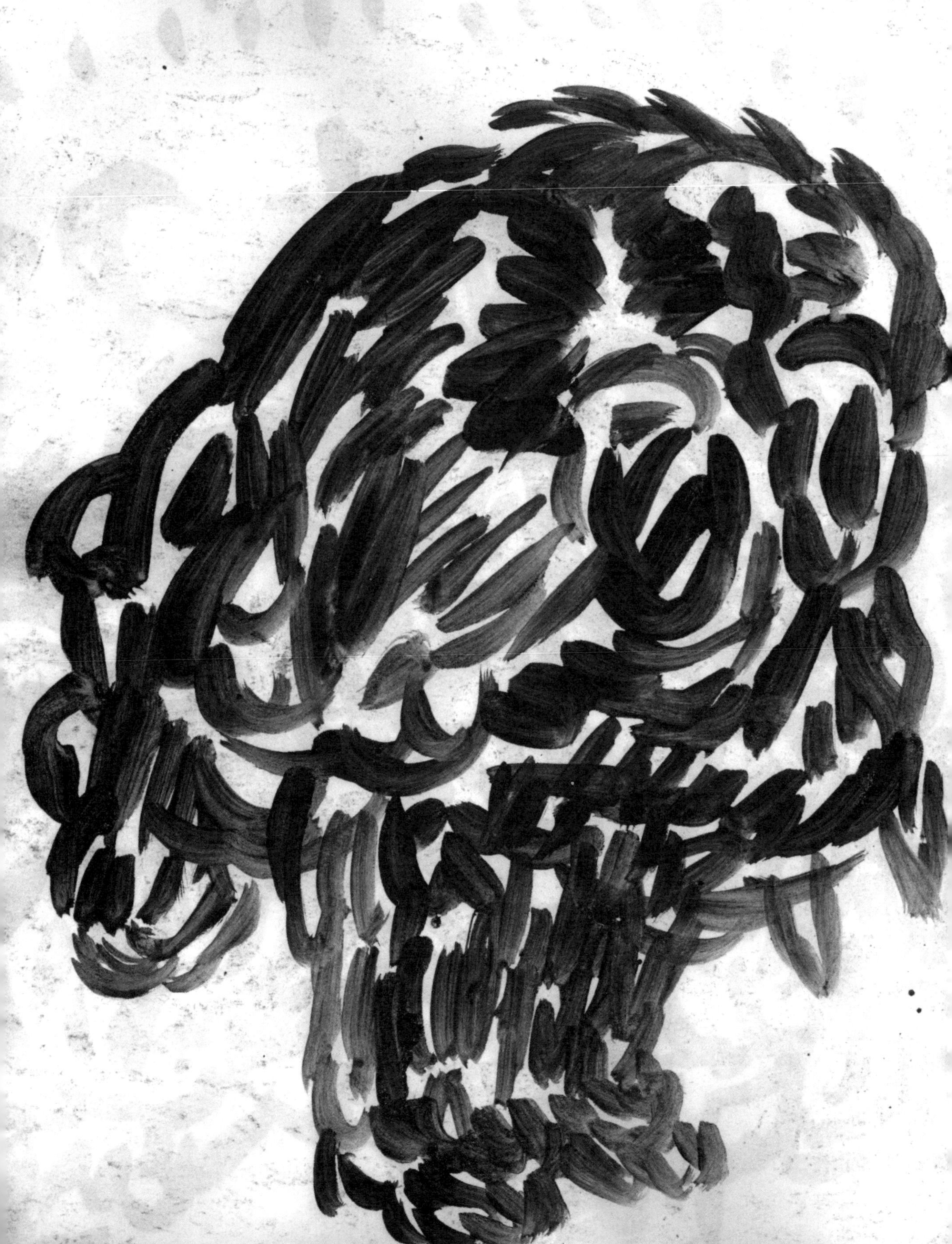

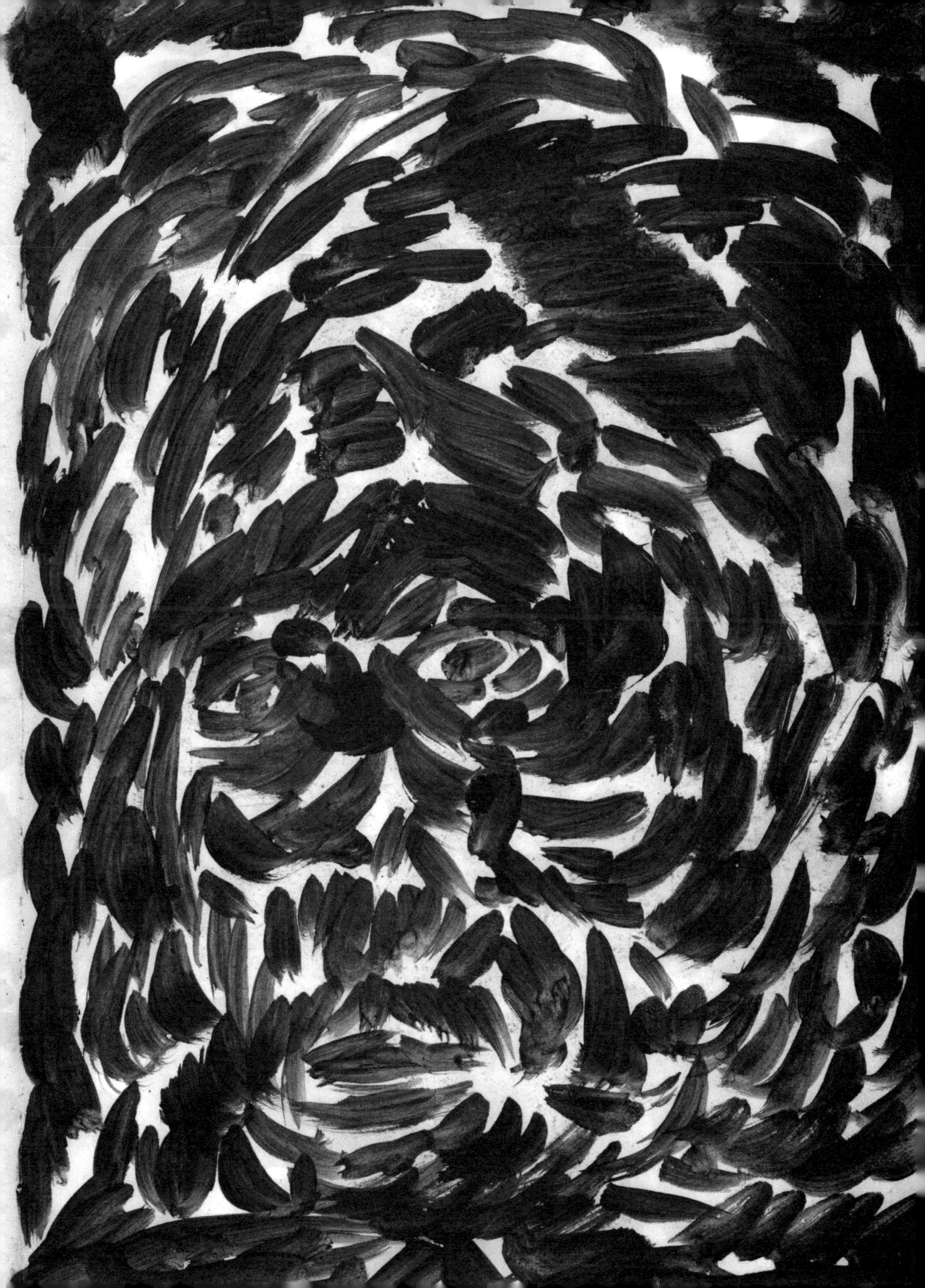

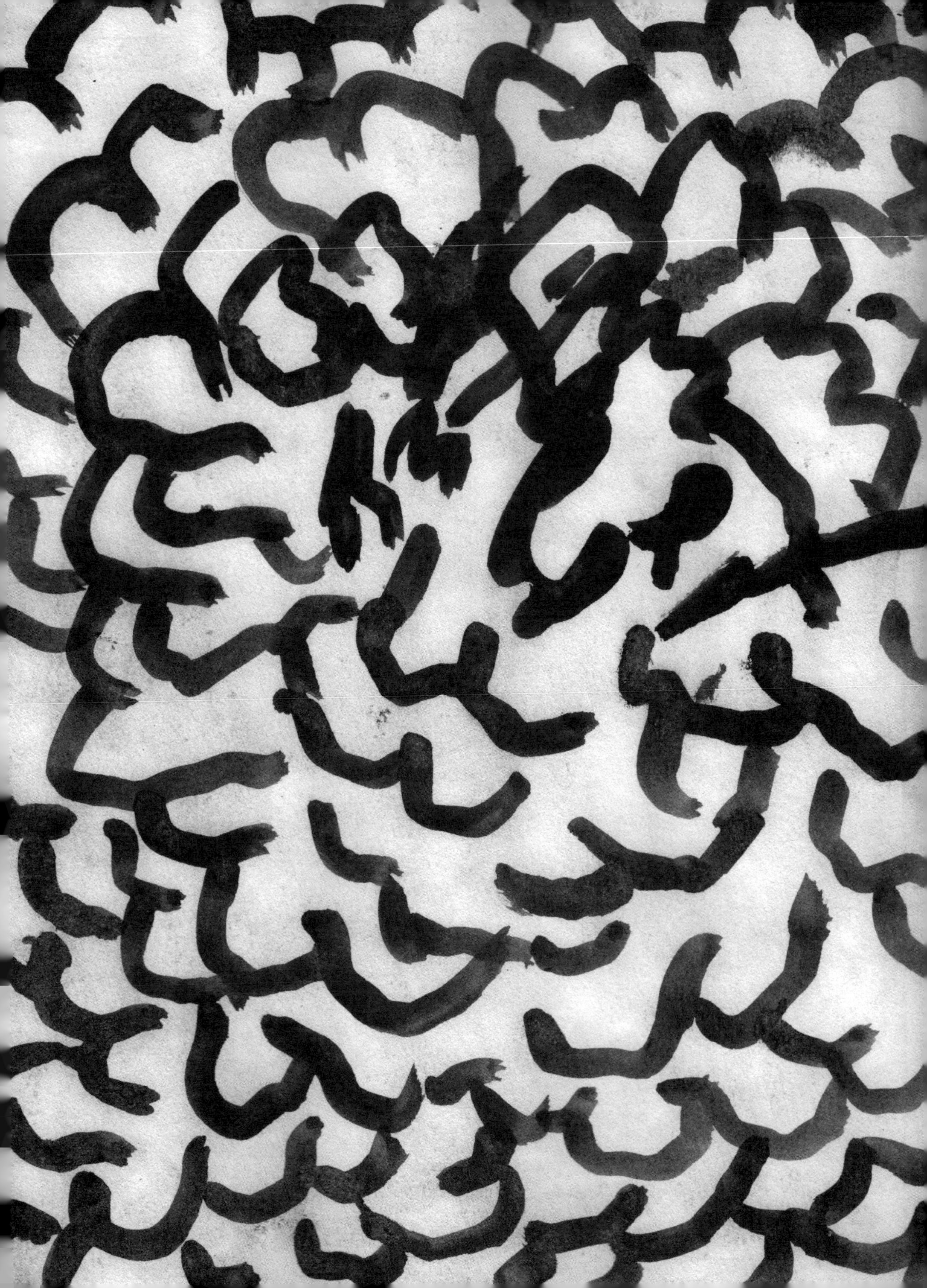

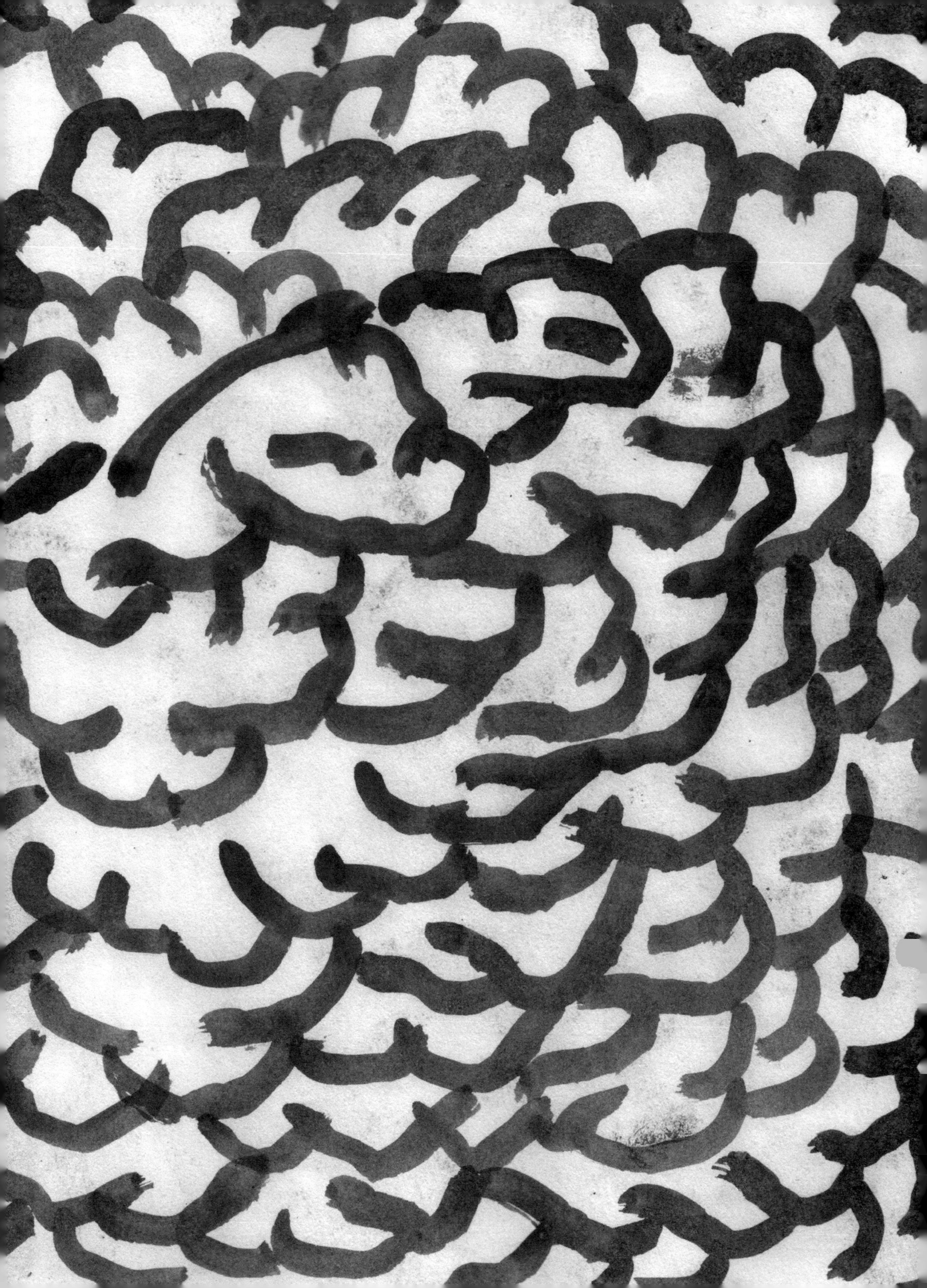

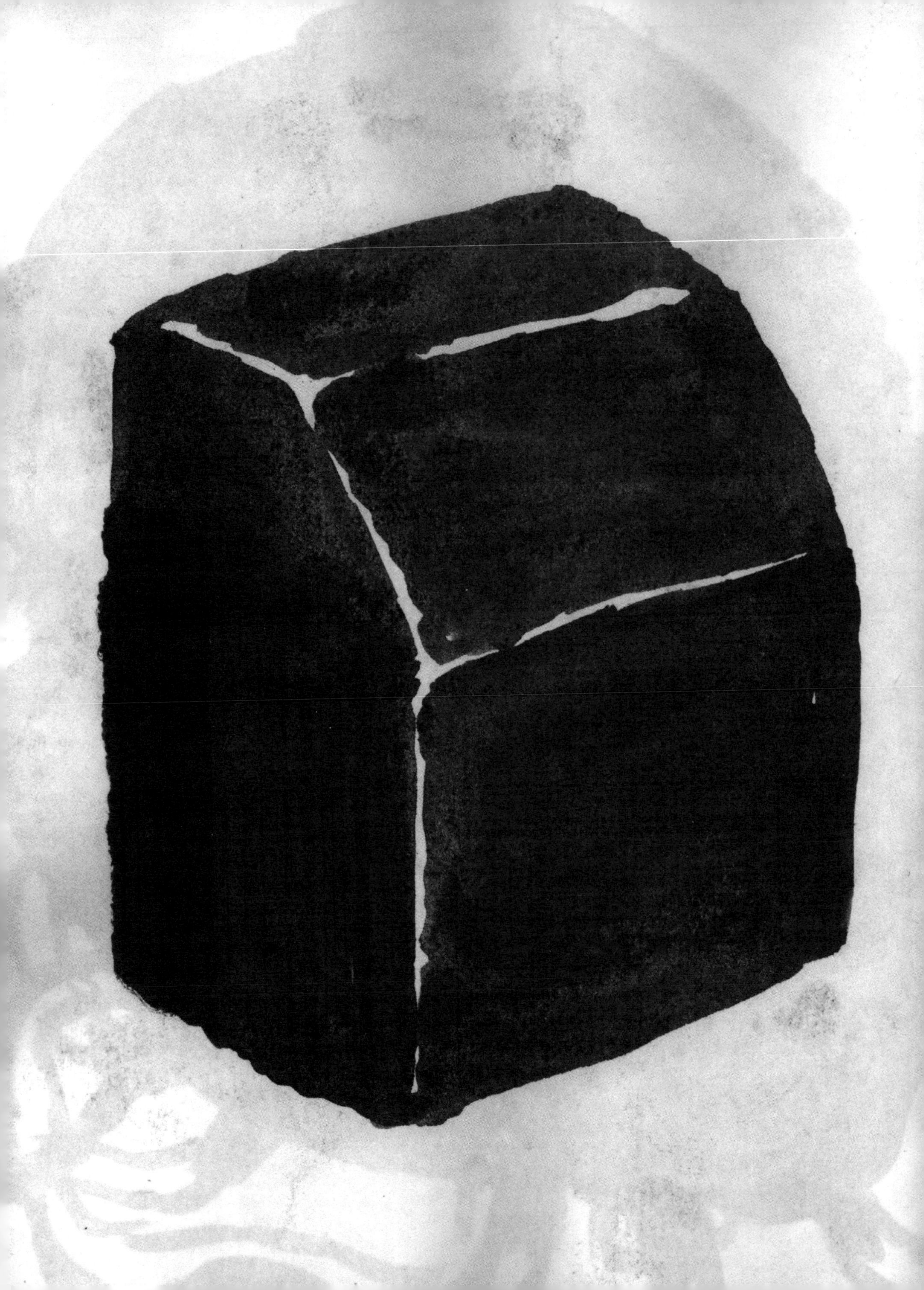

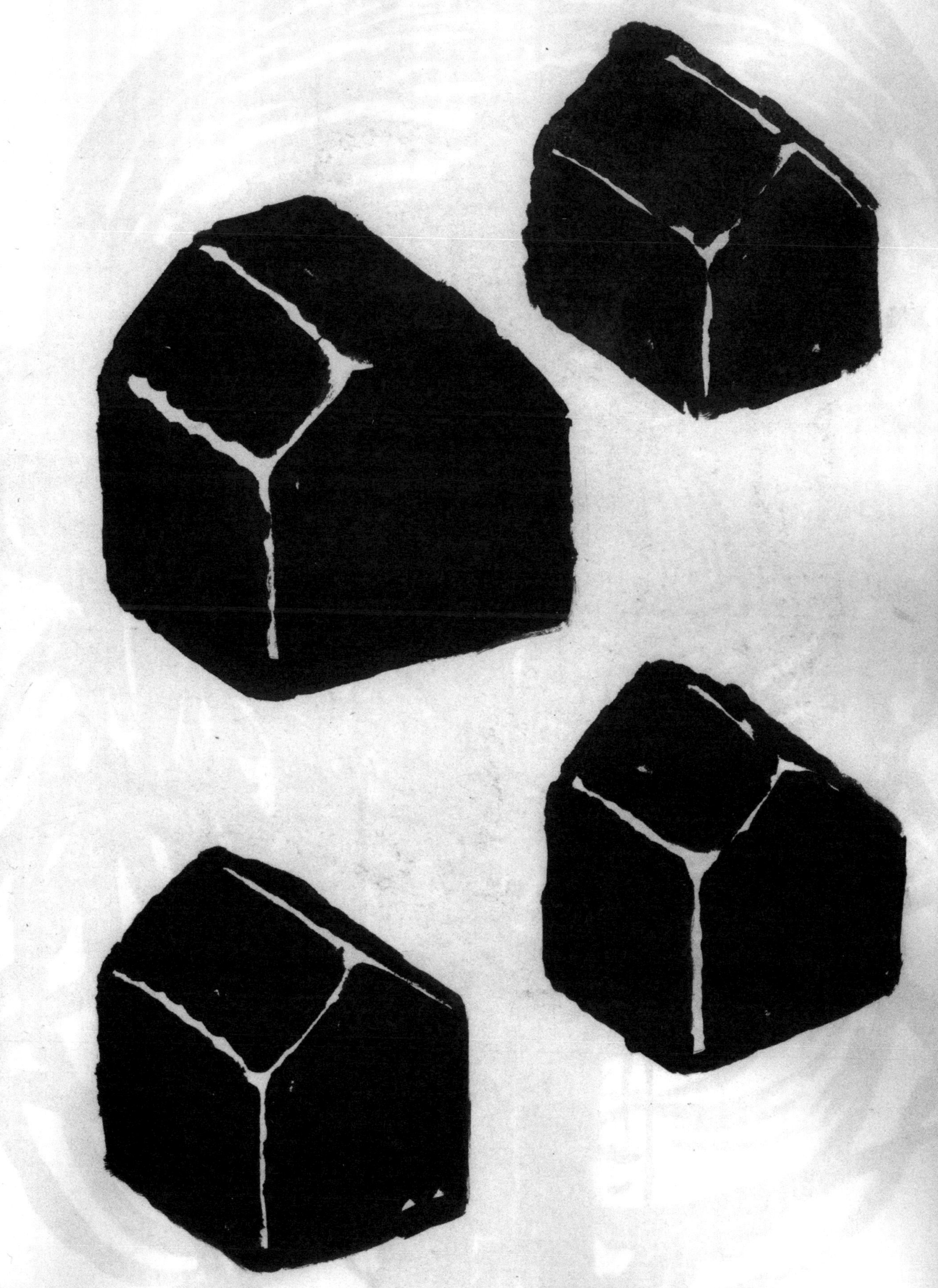

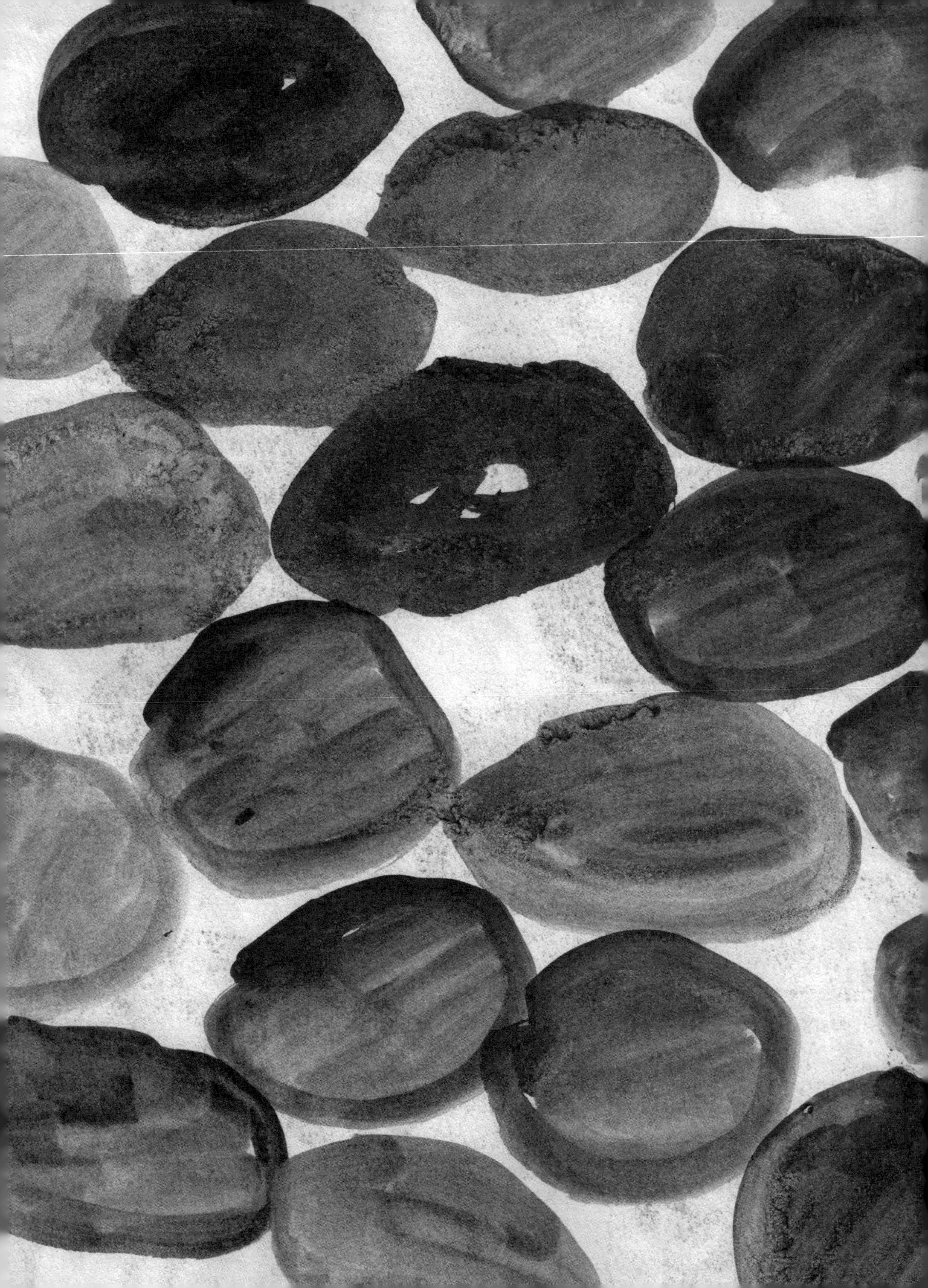

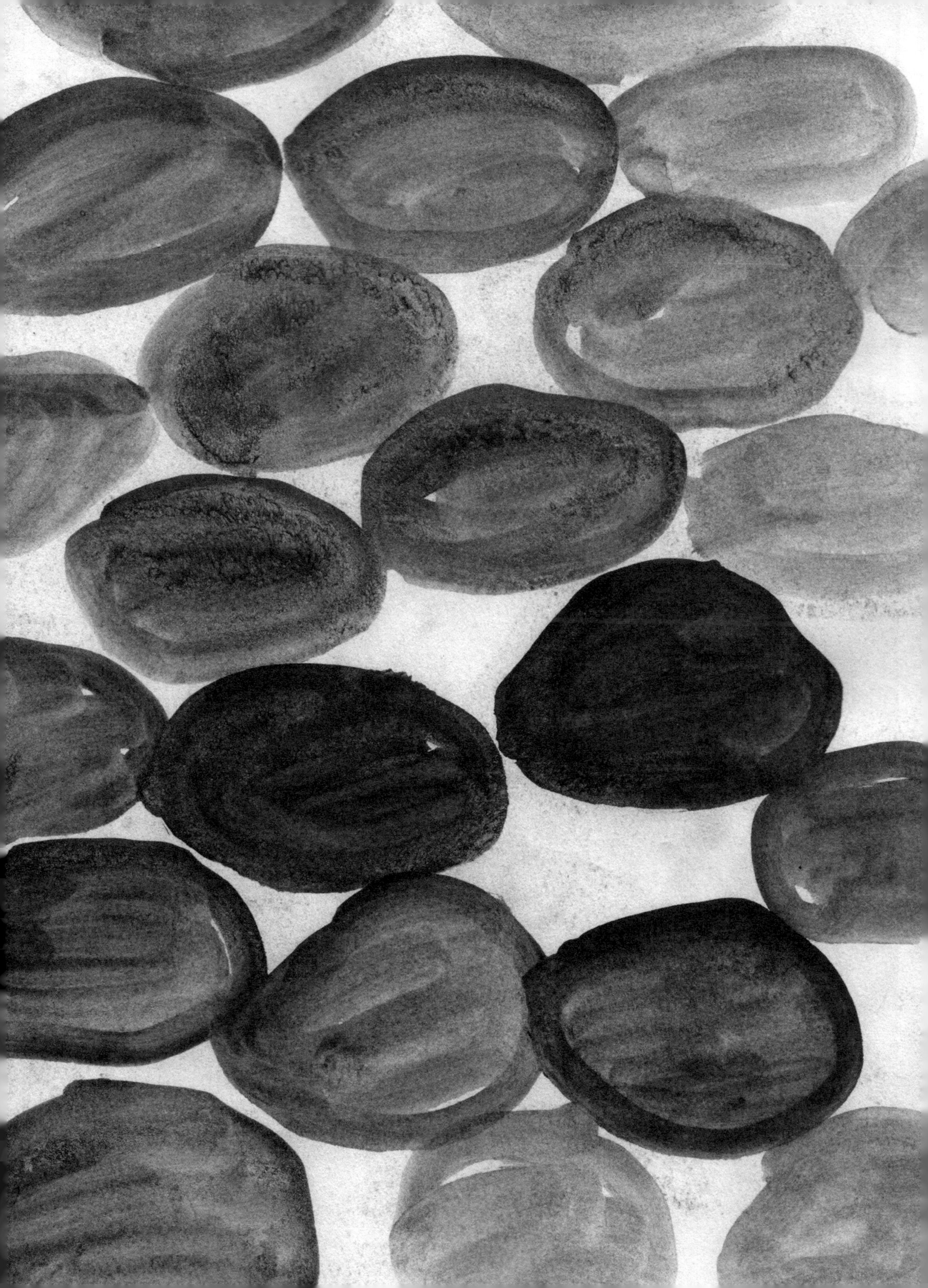

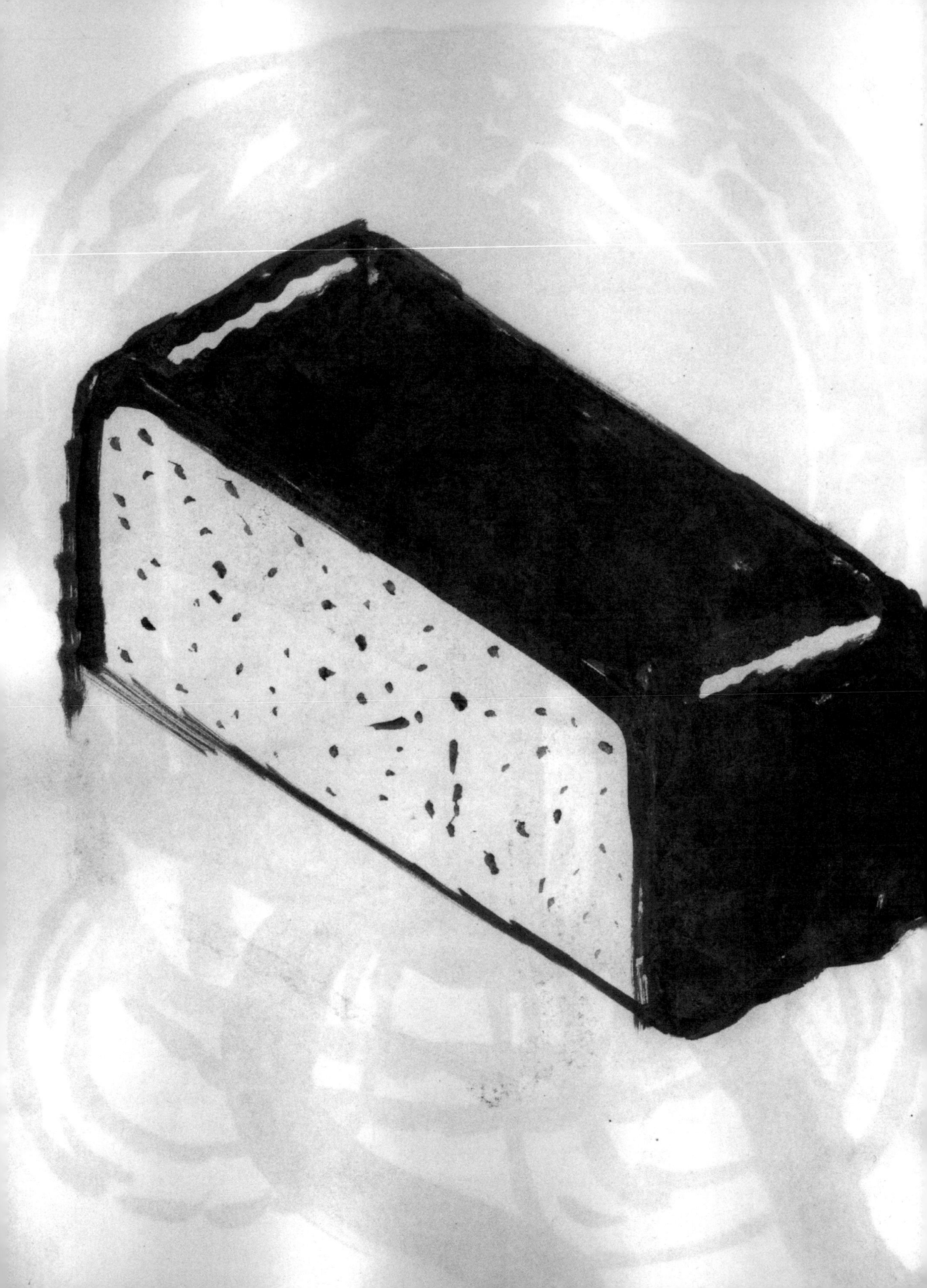

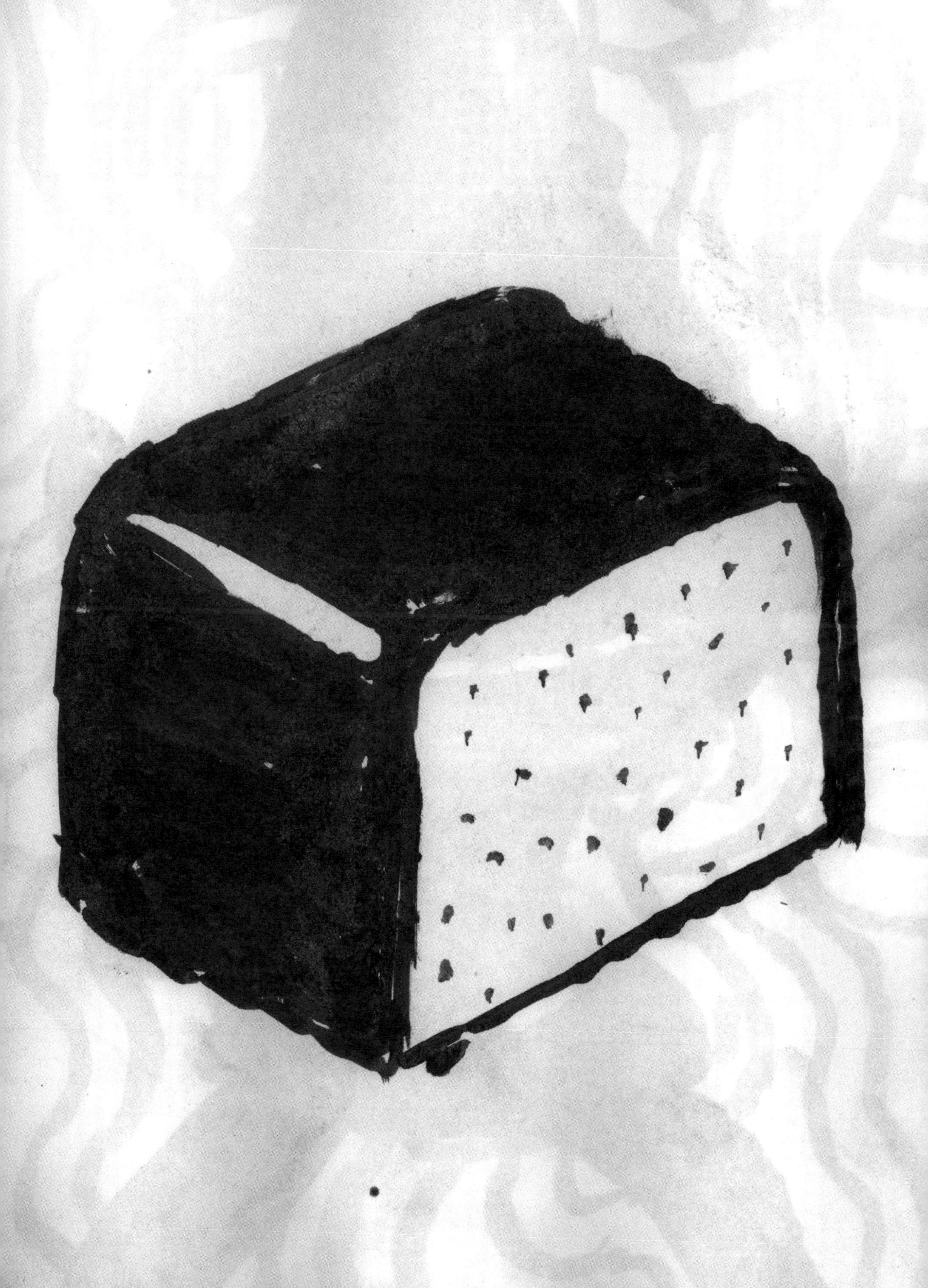

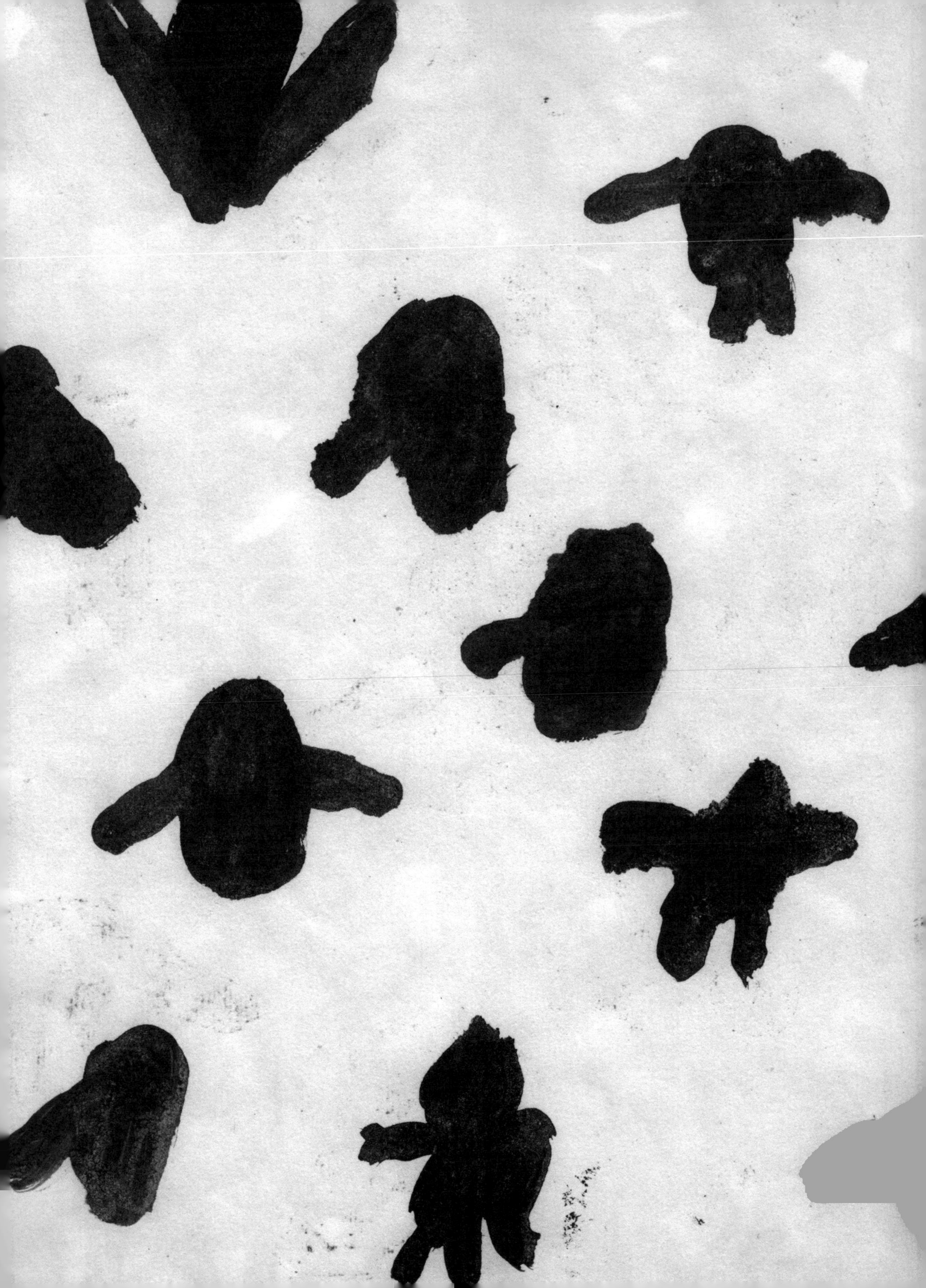

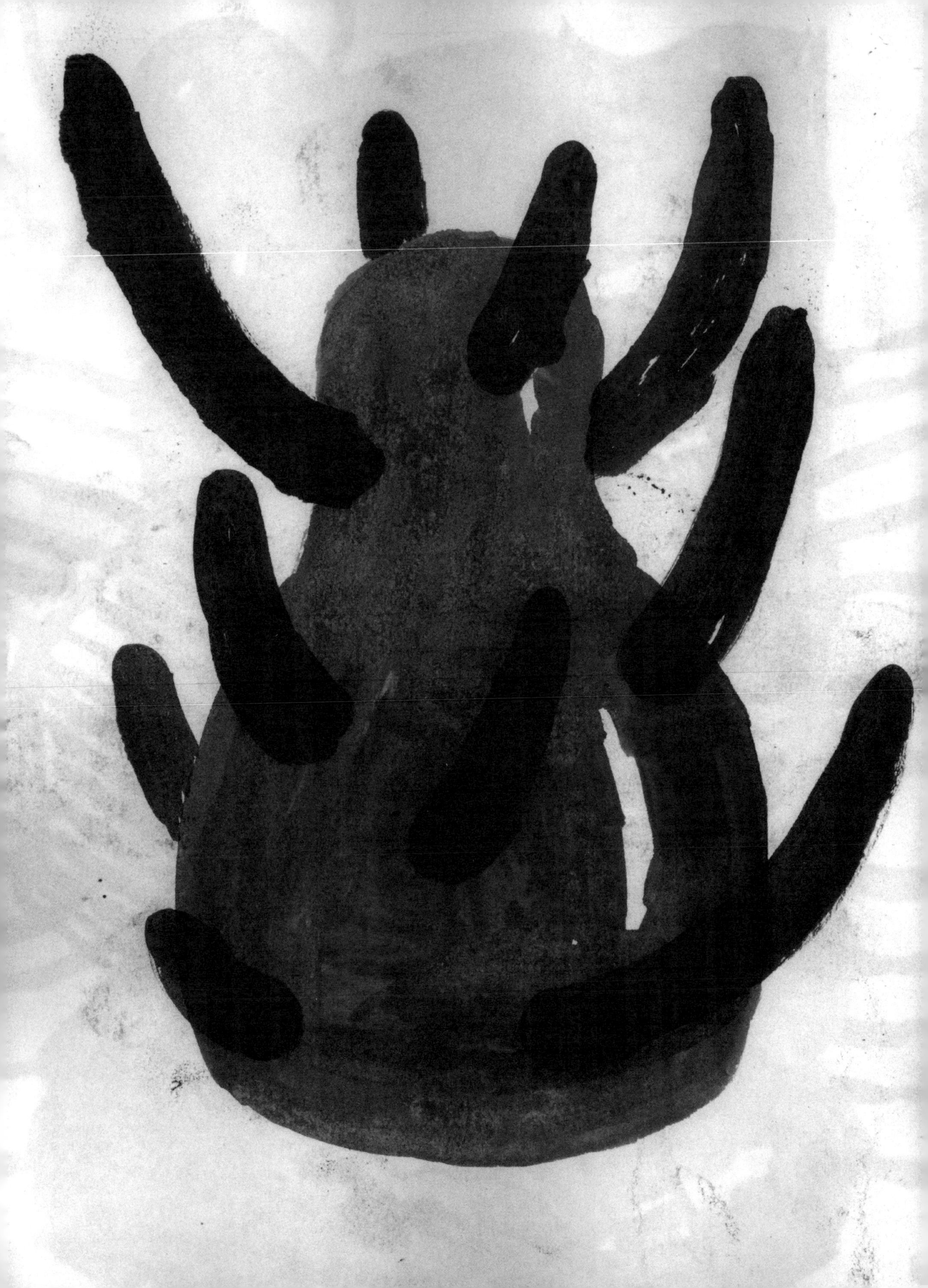

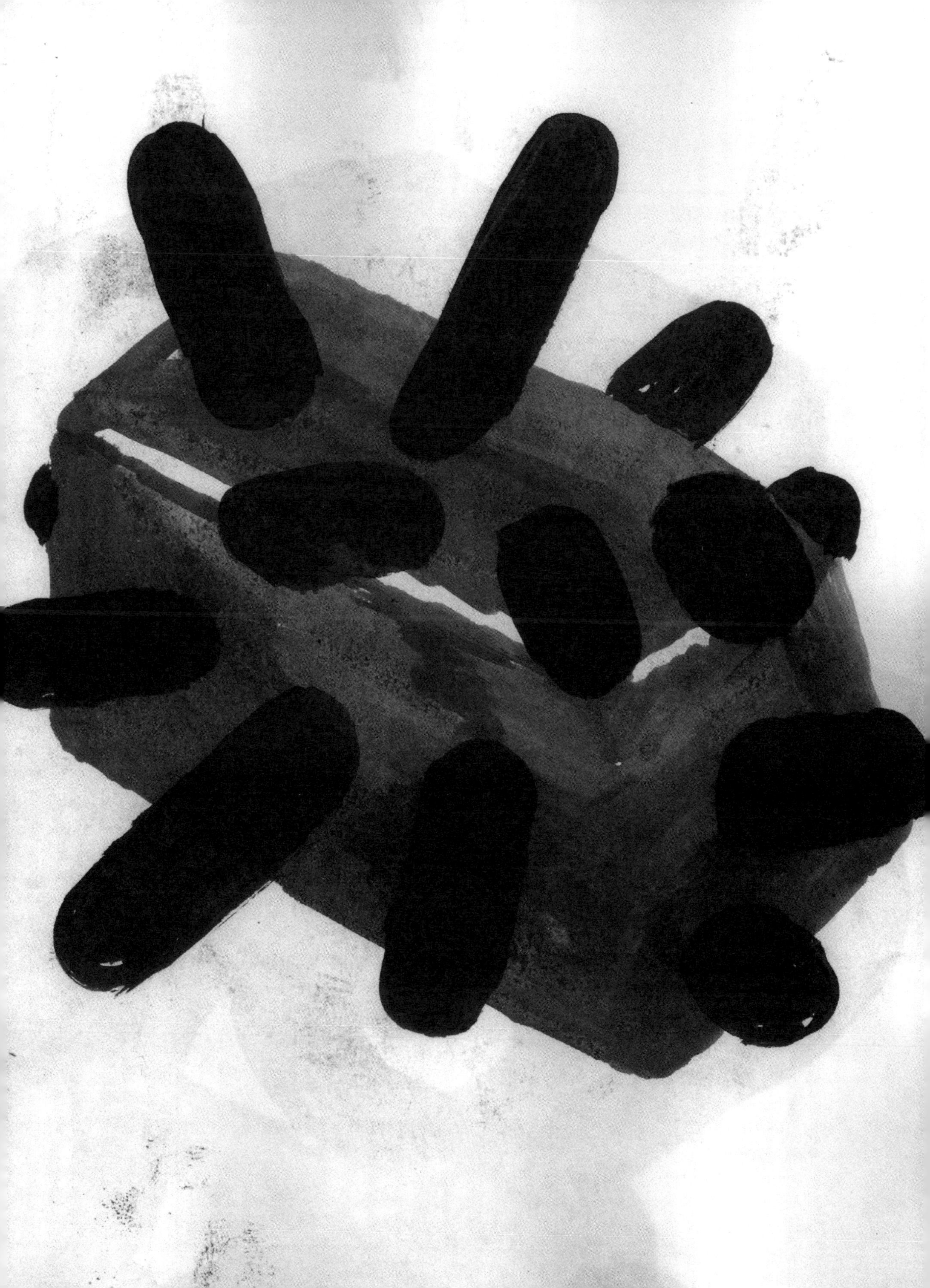

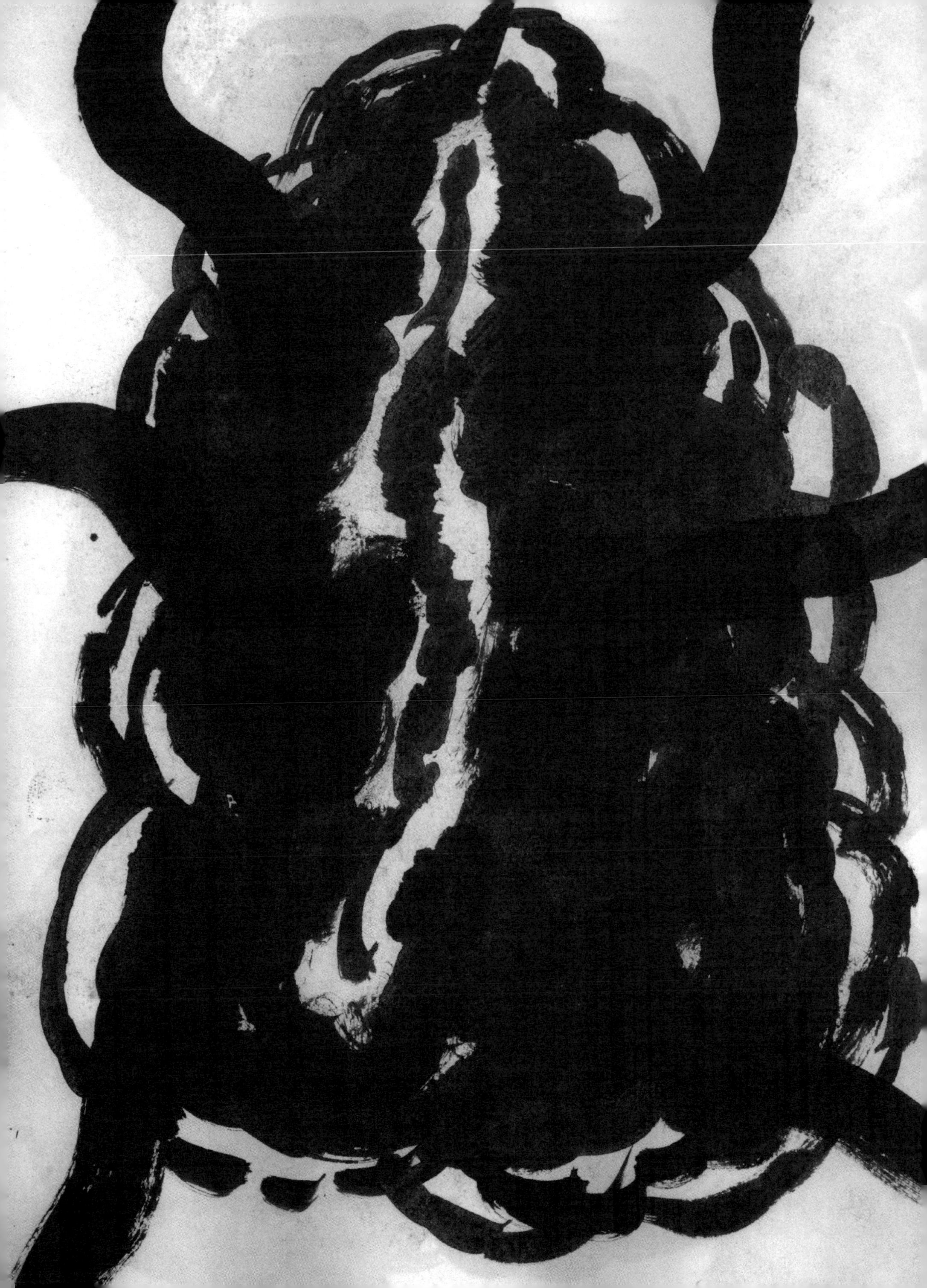

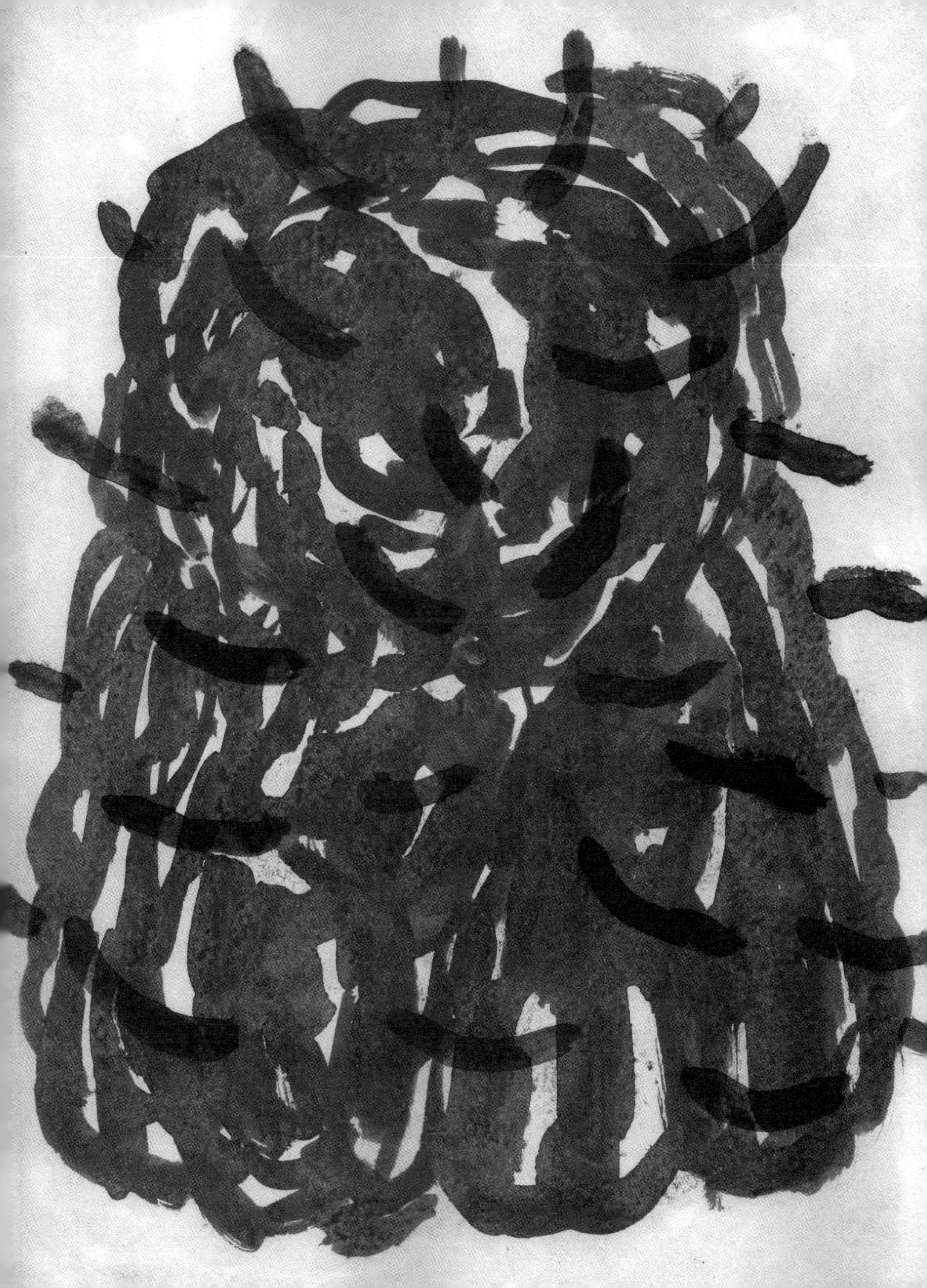

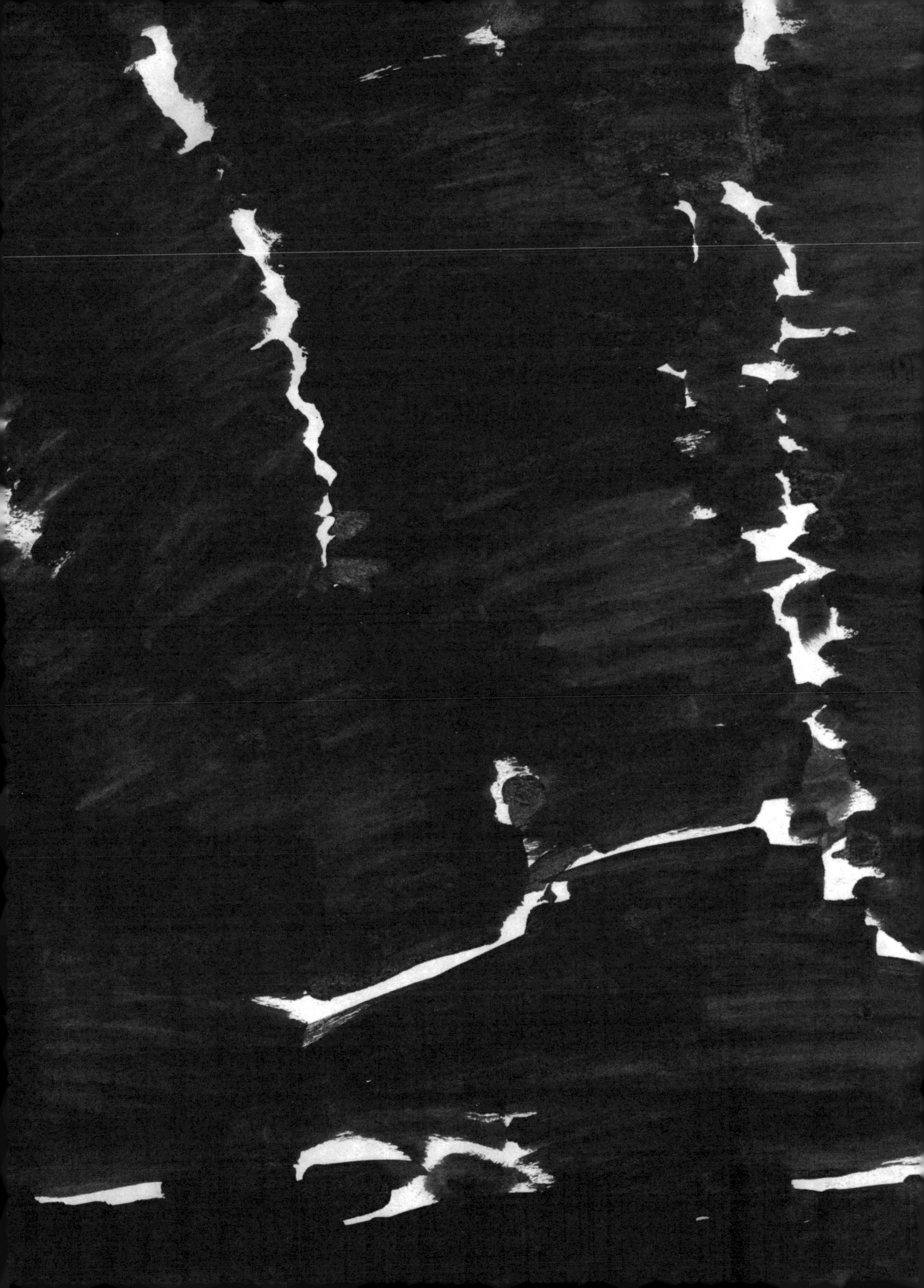

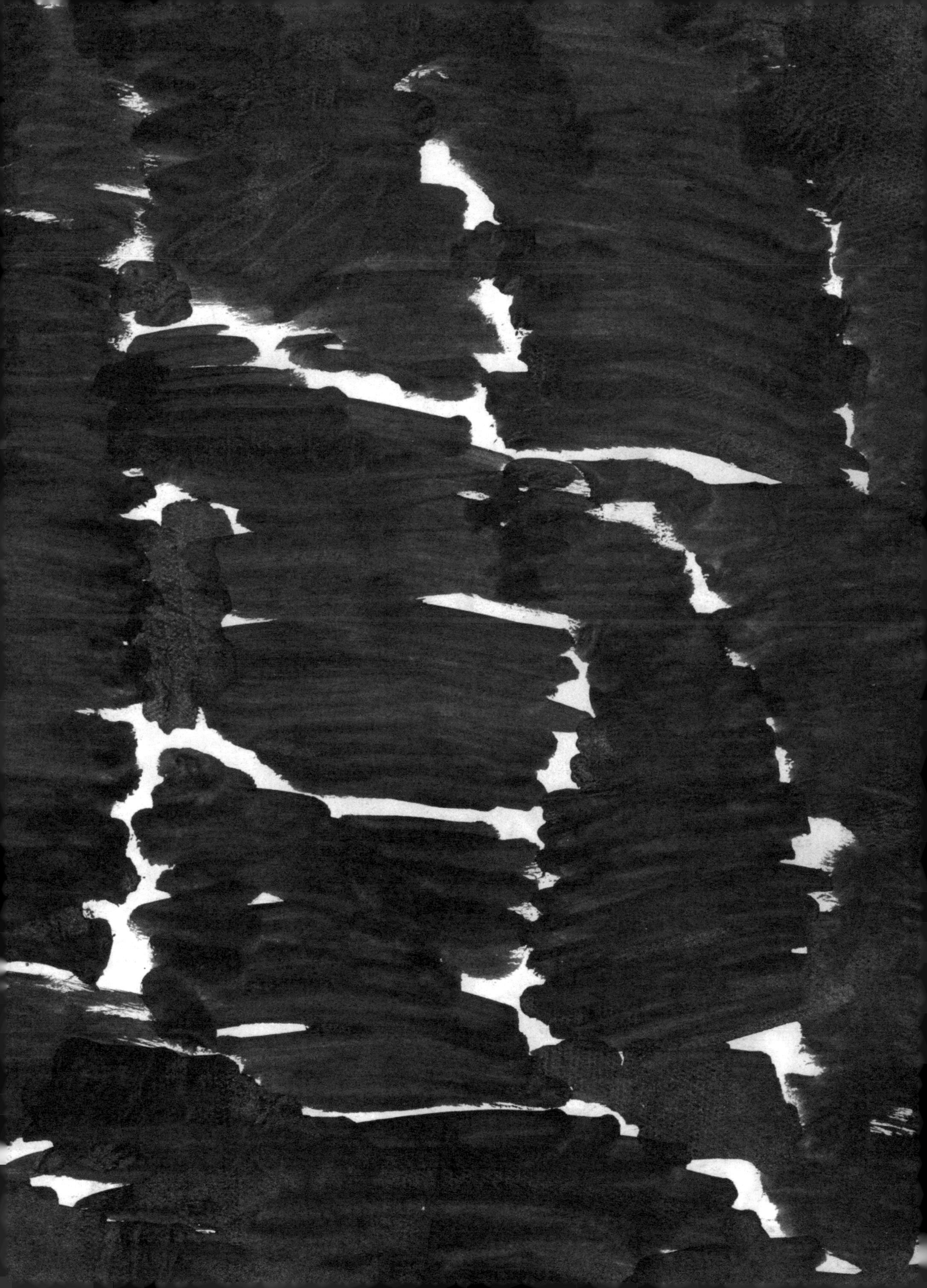

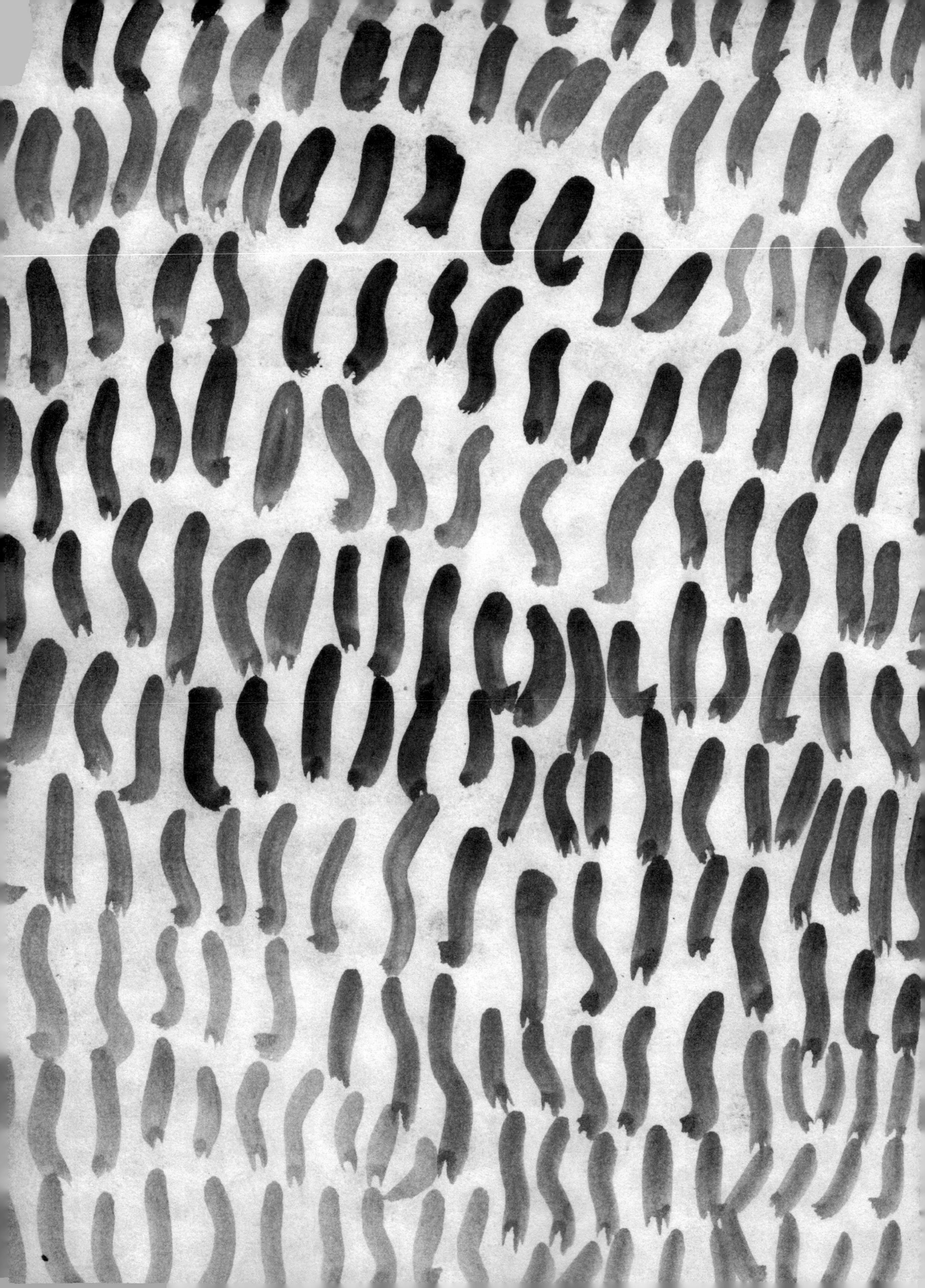

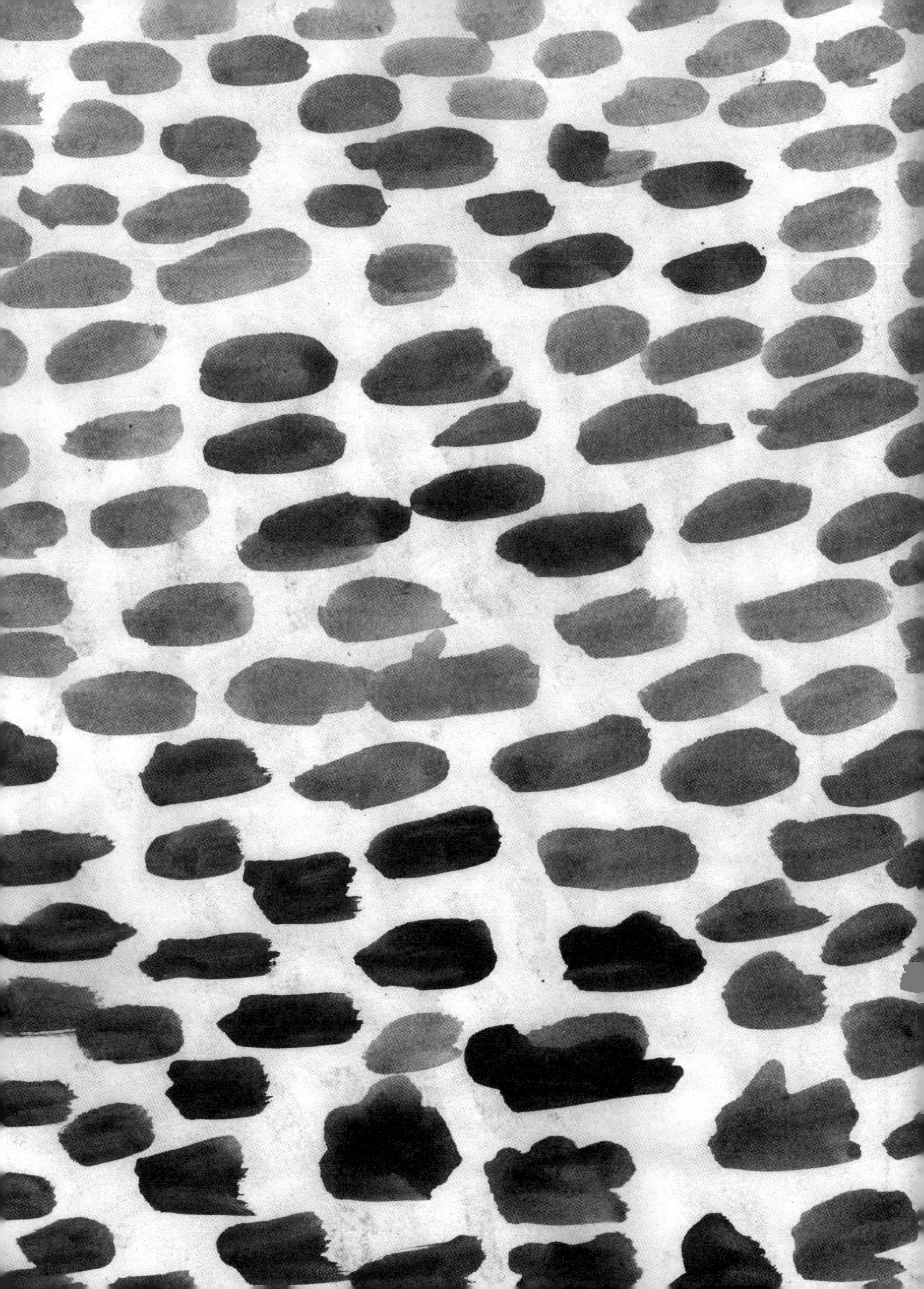

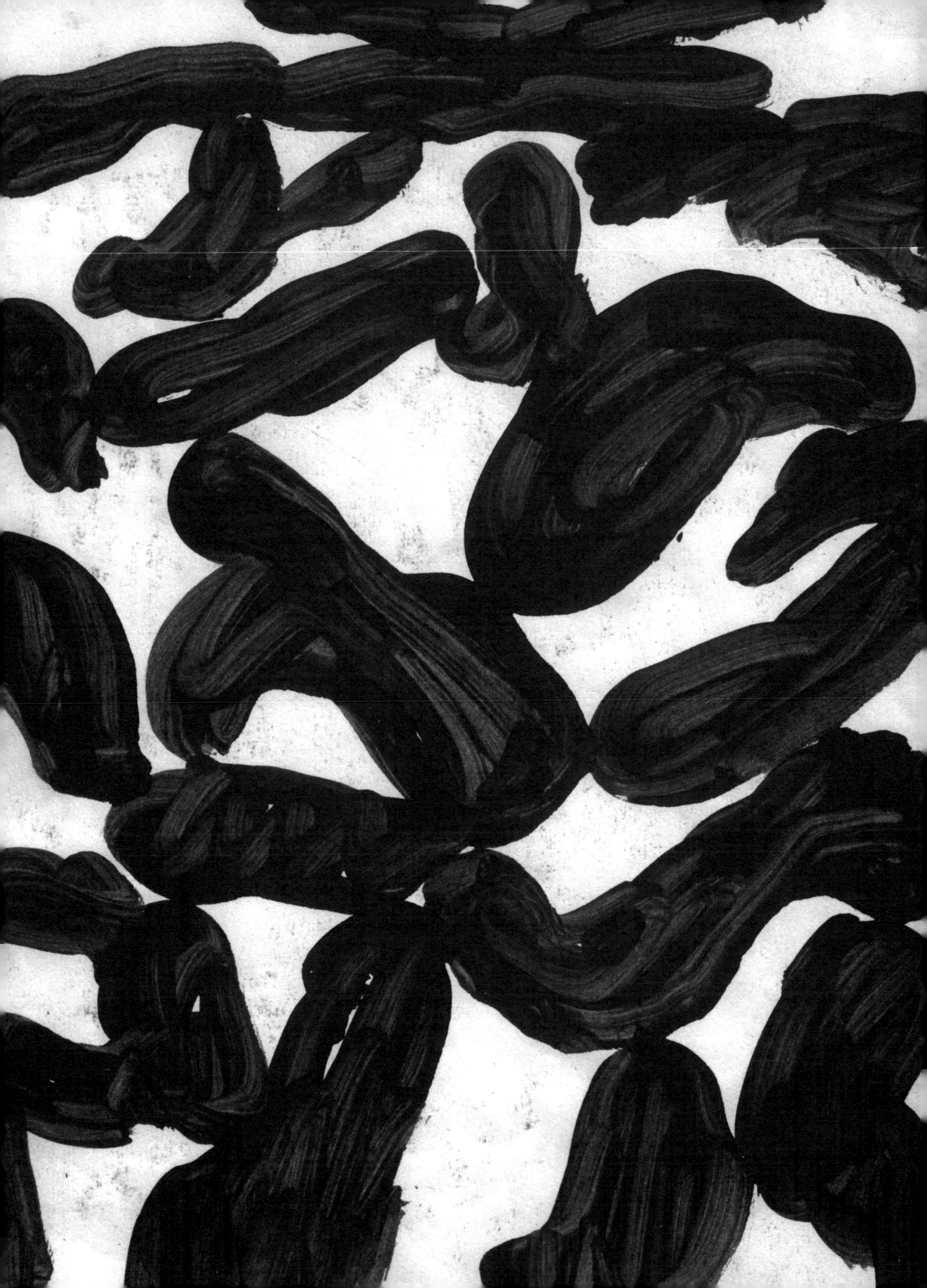

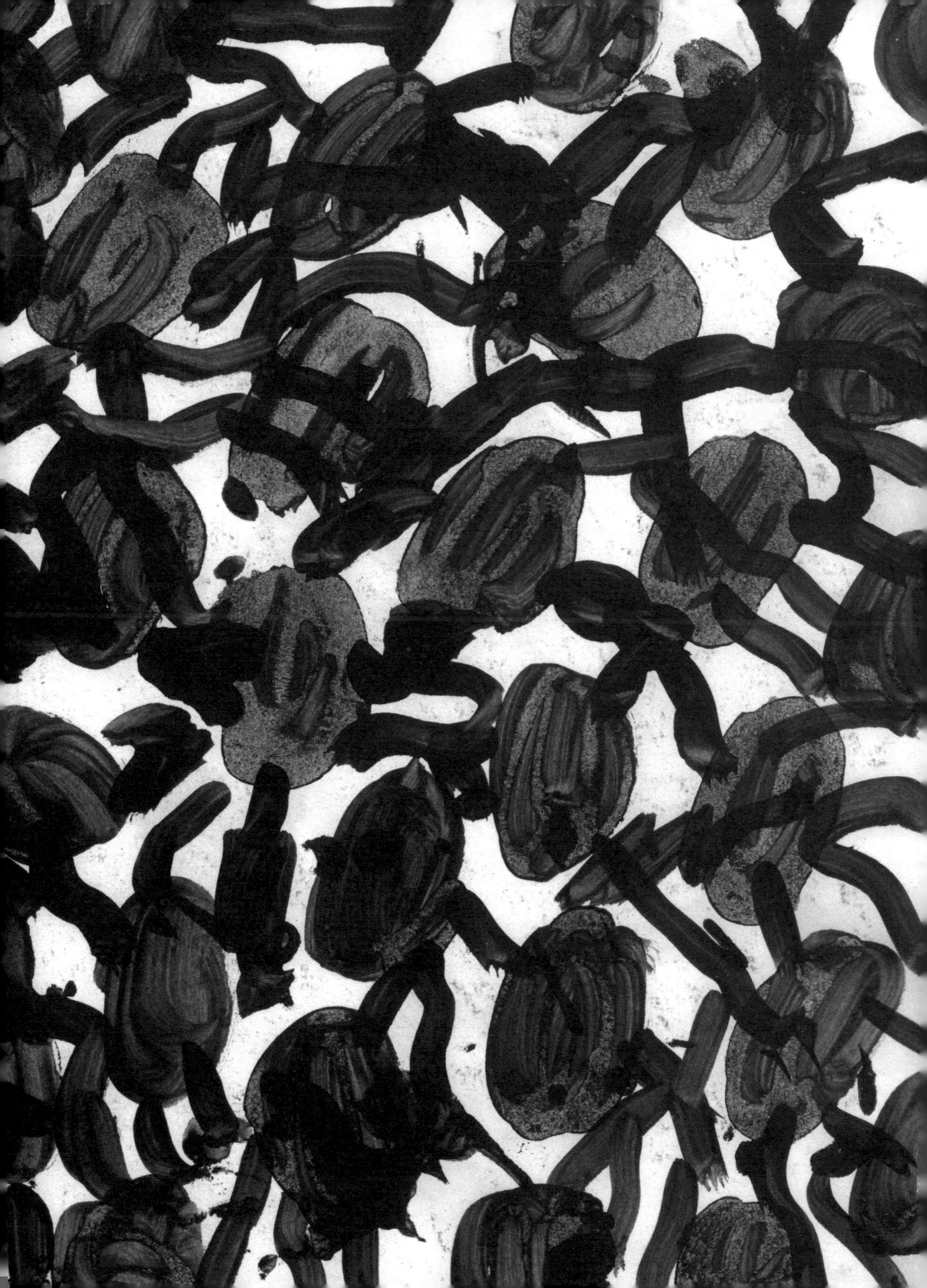

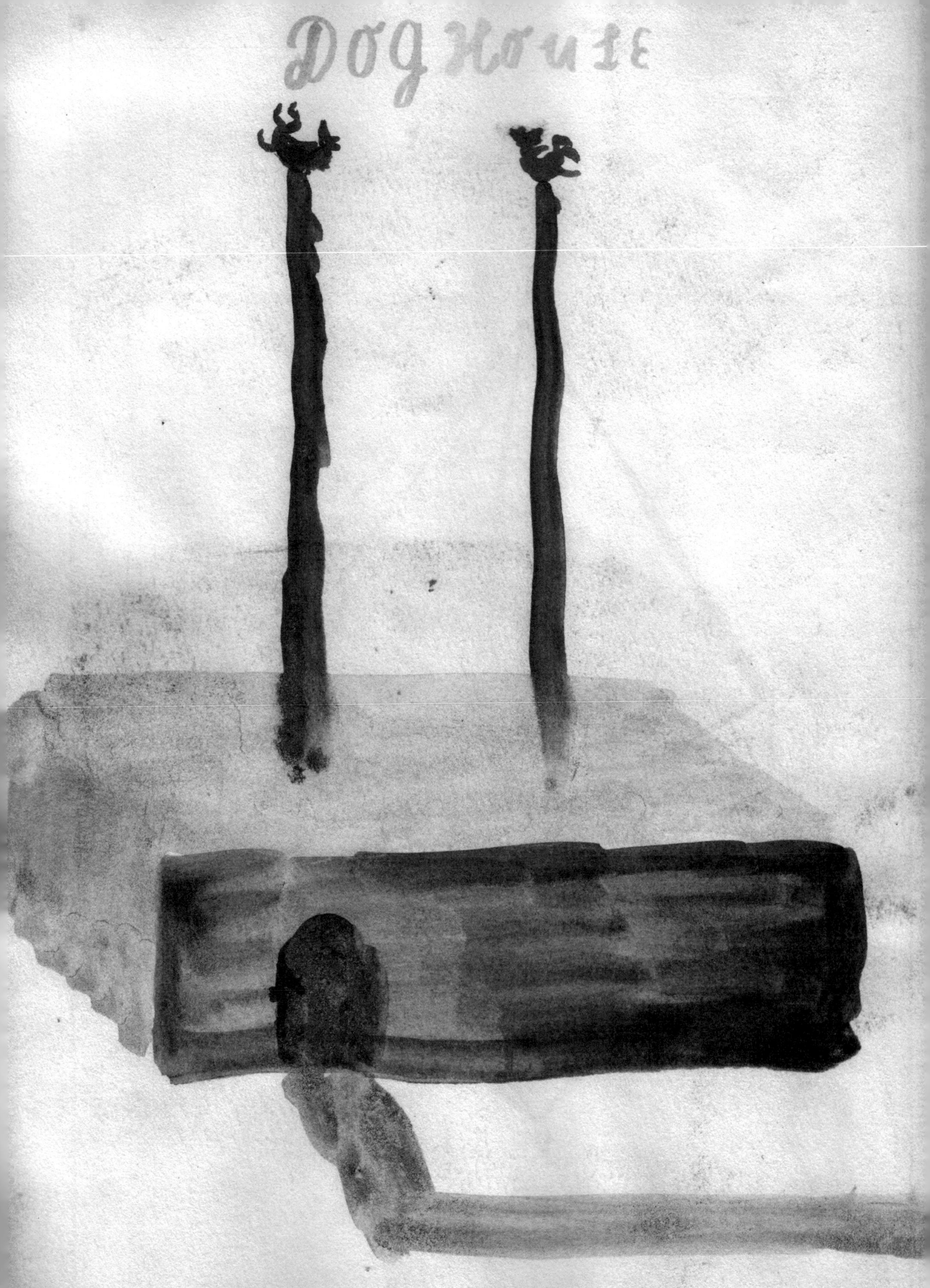
DogHouse

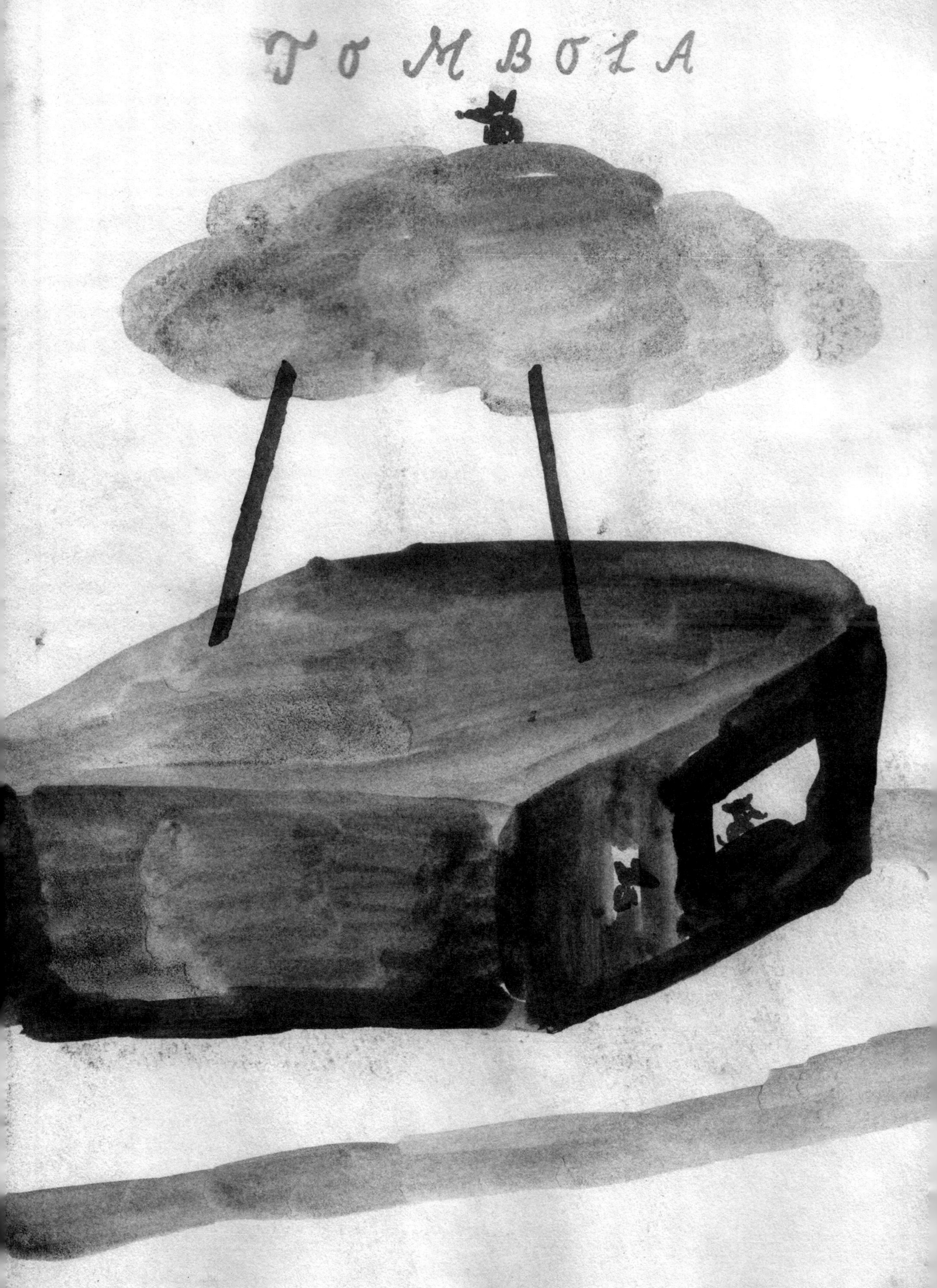
TOMBOLA

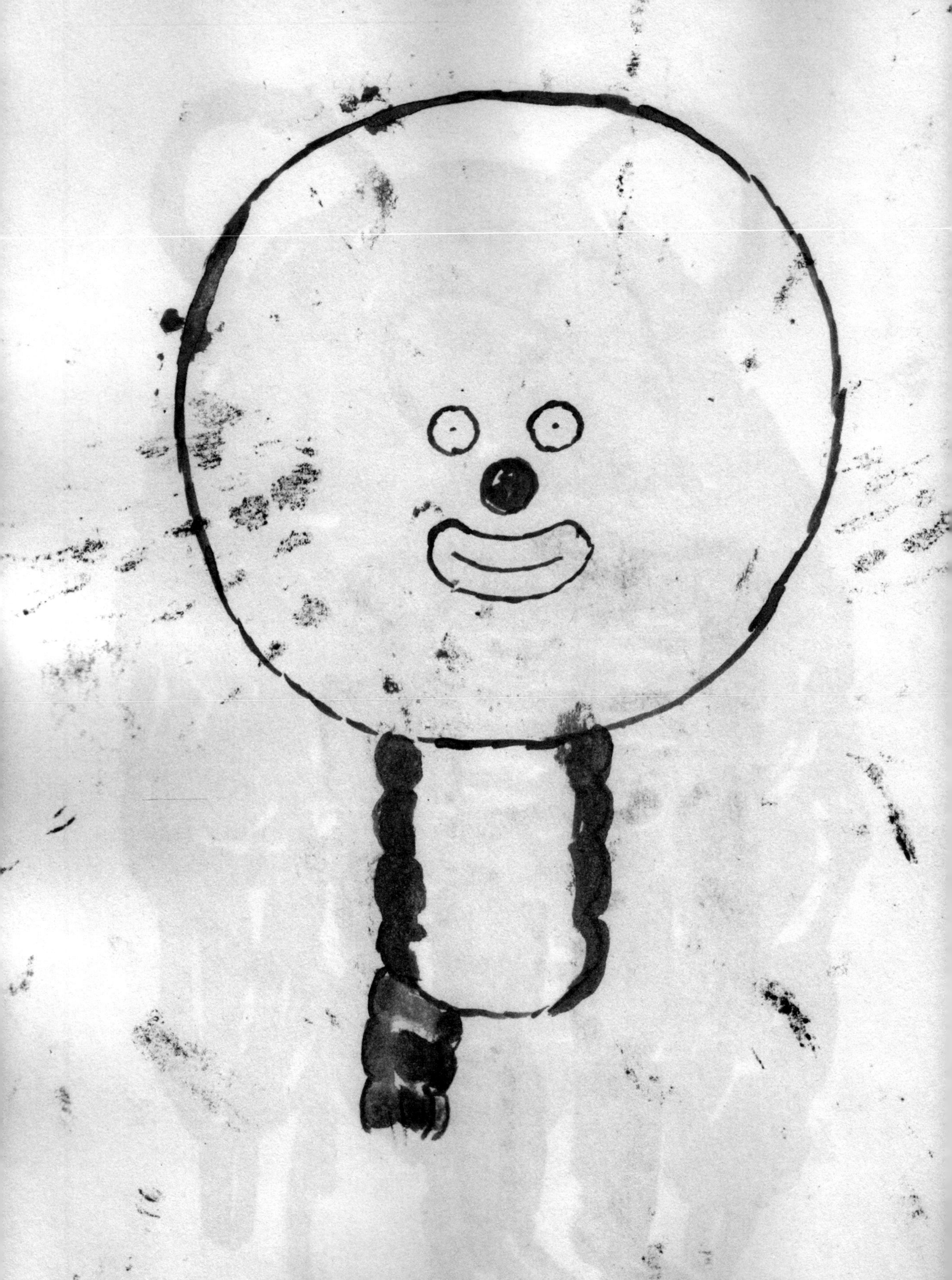

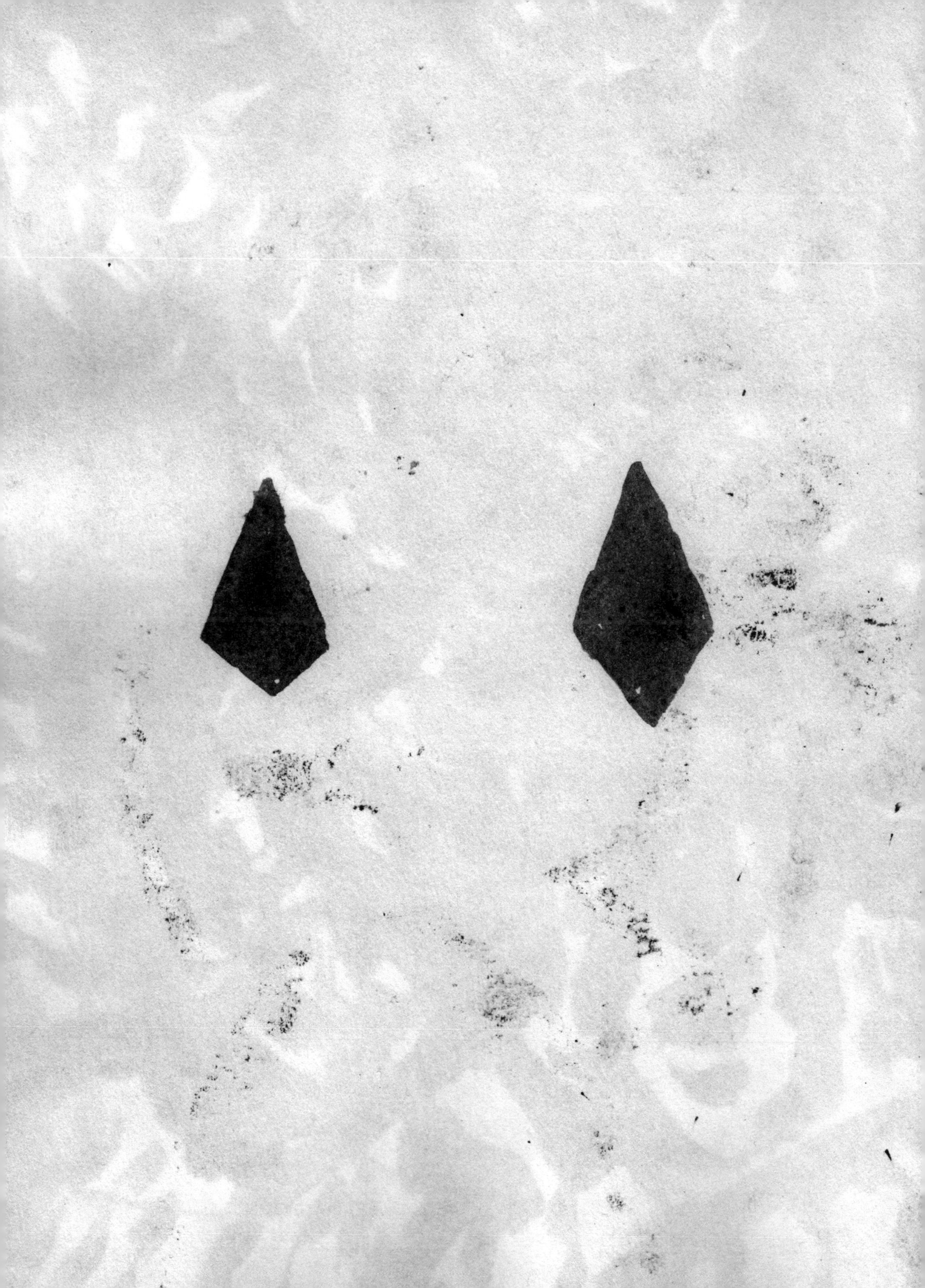

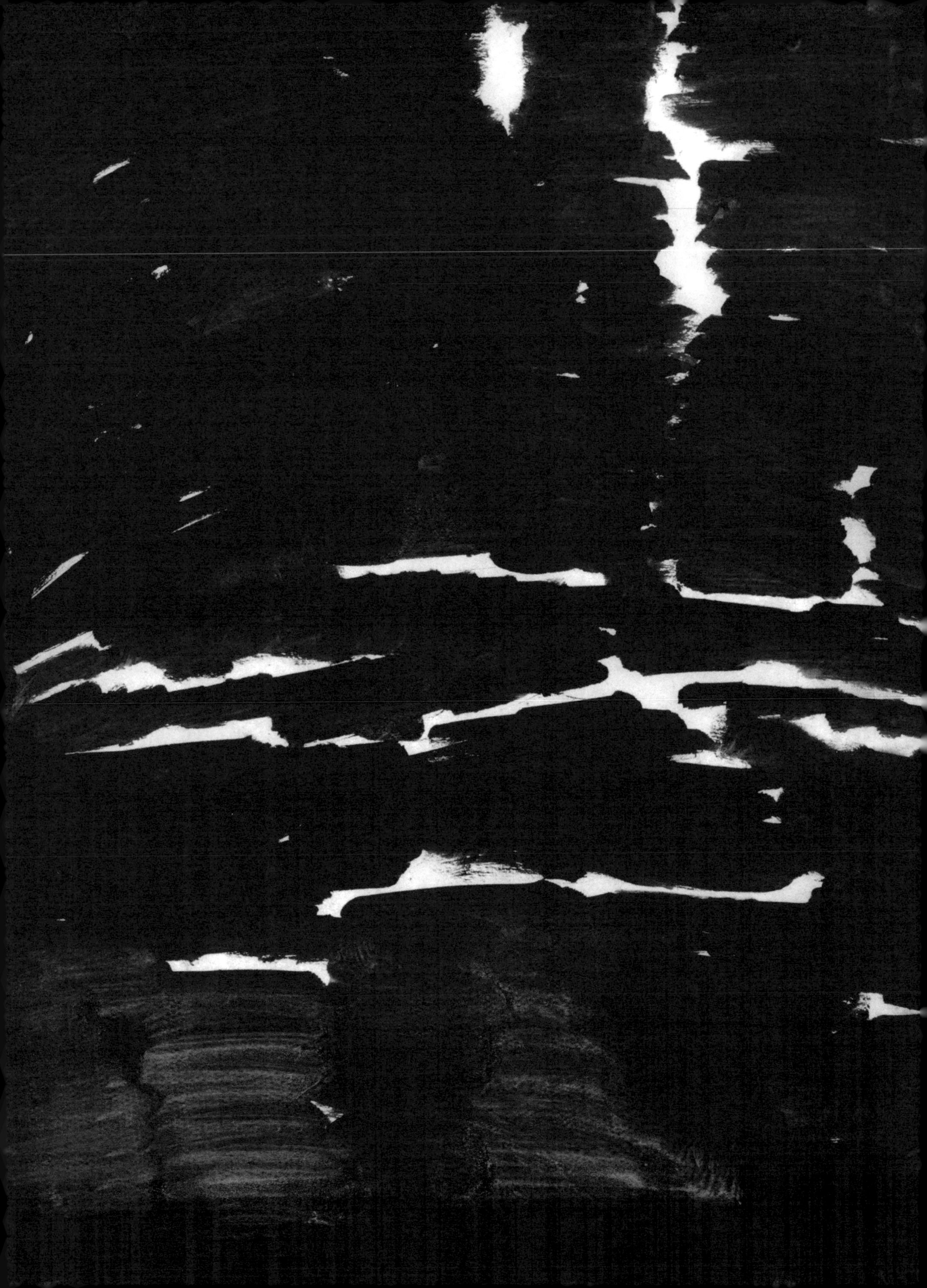

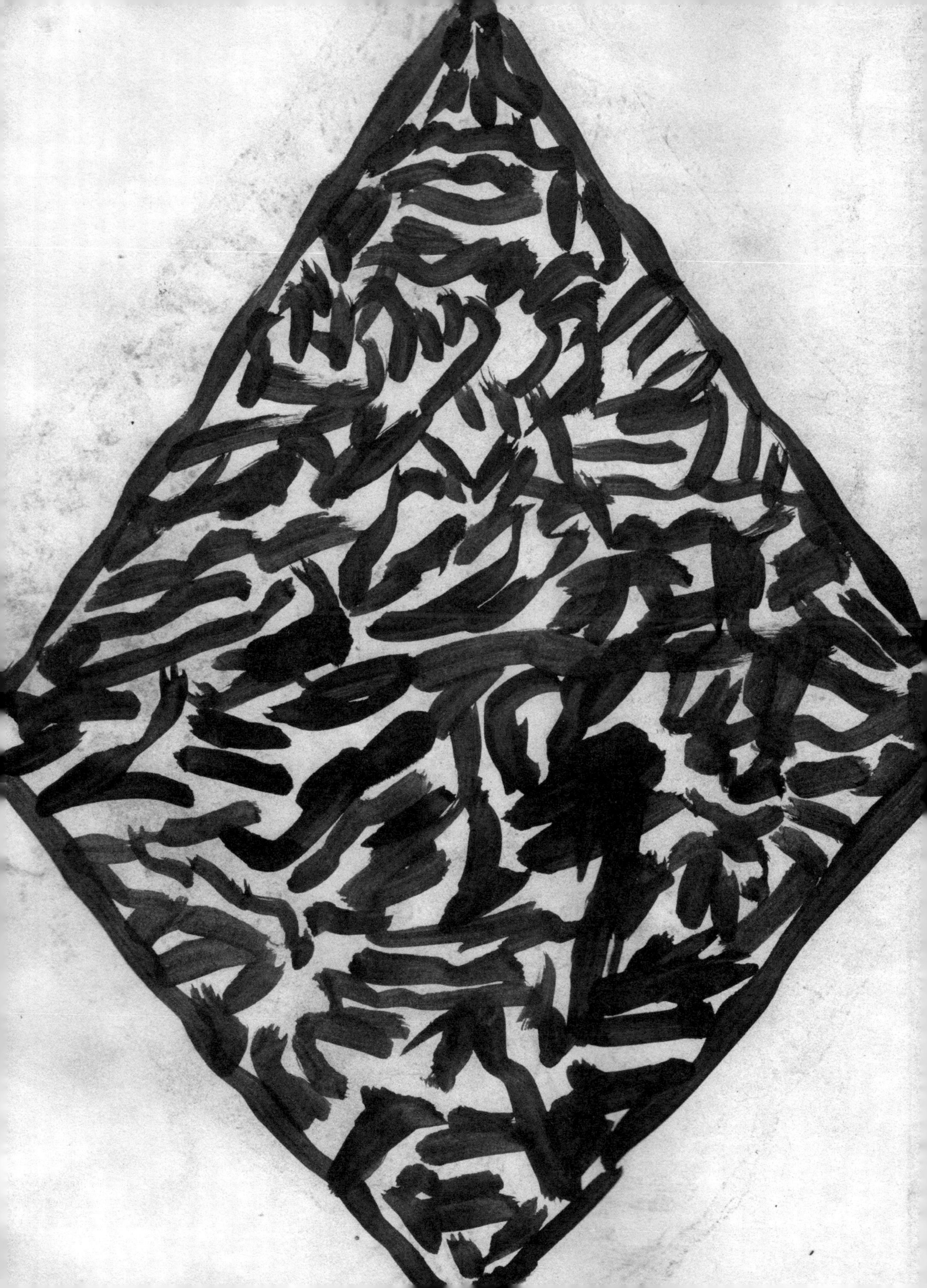

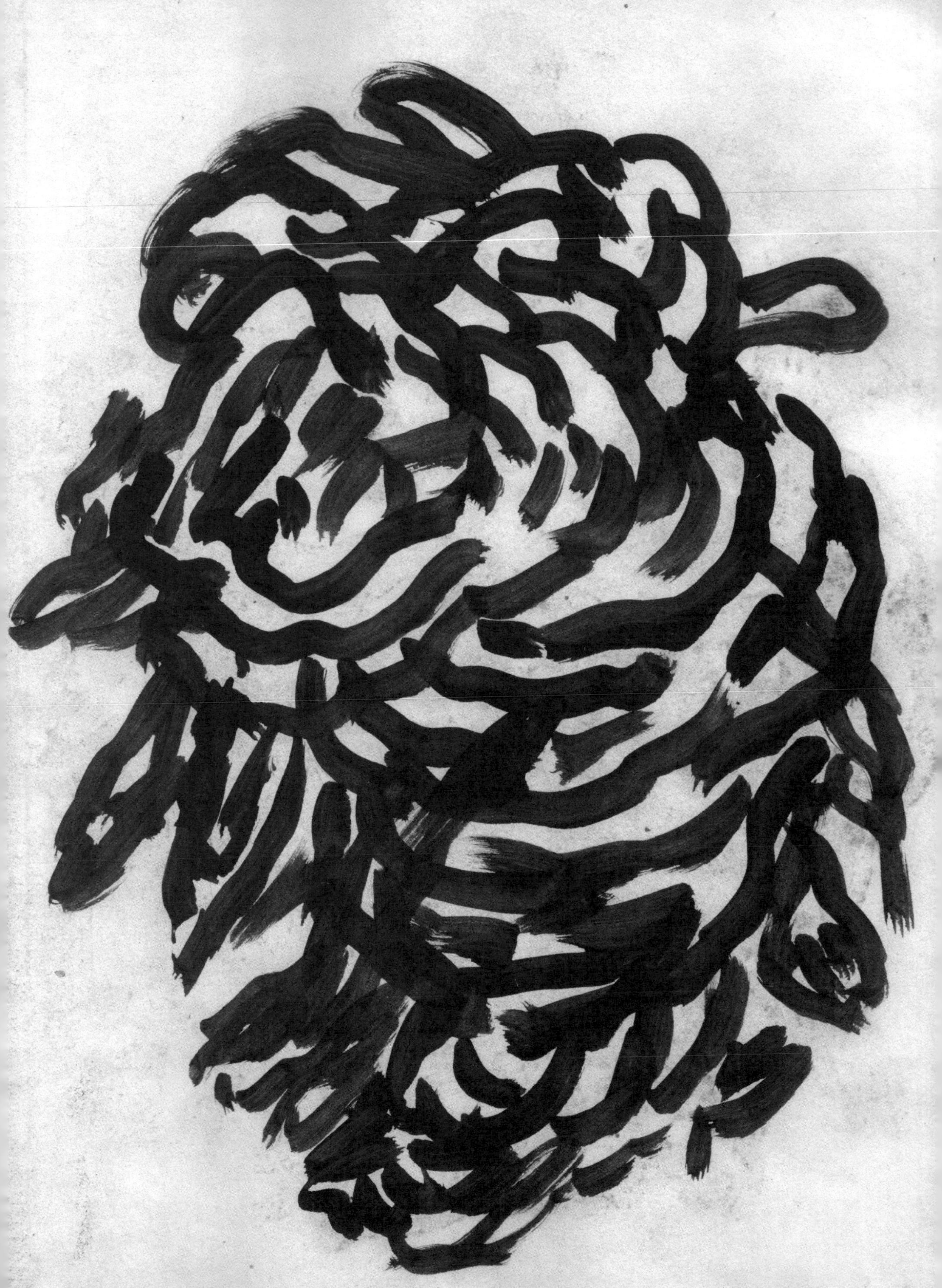

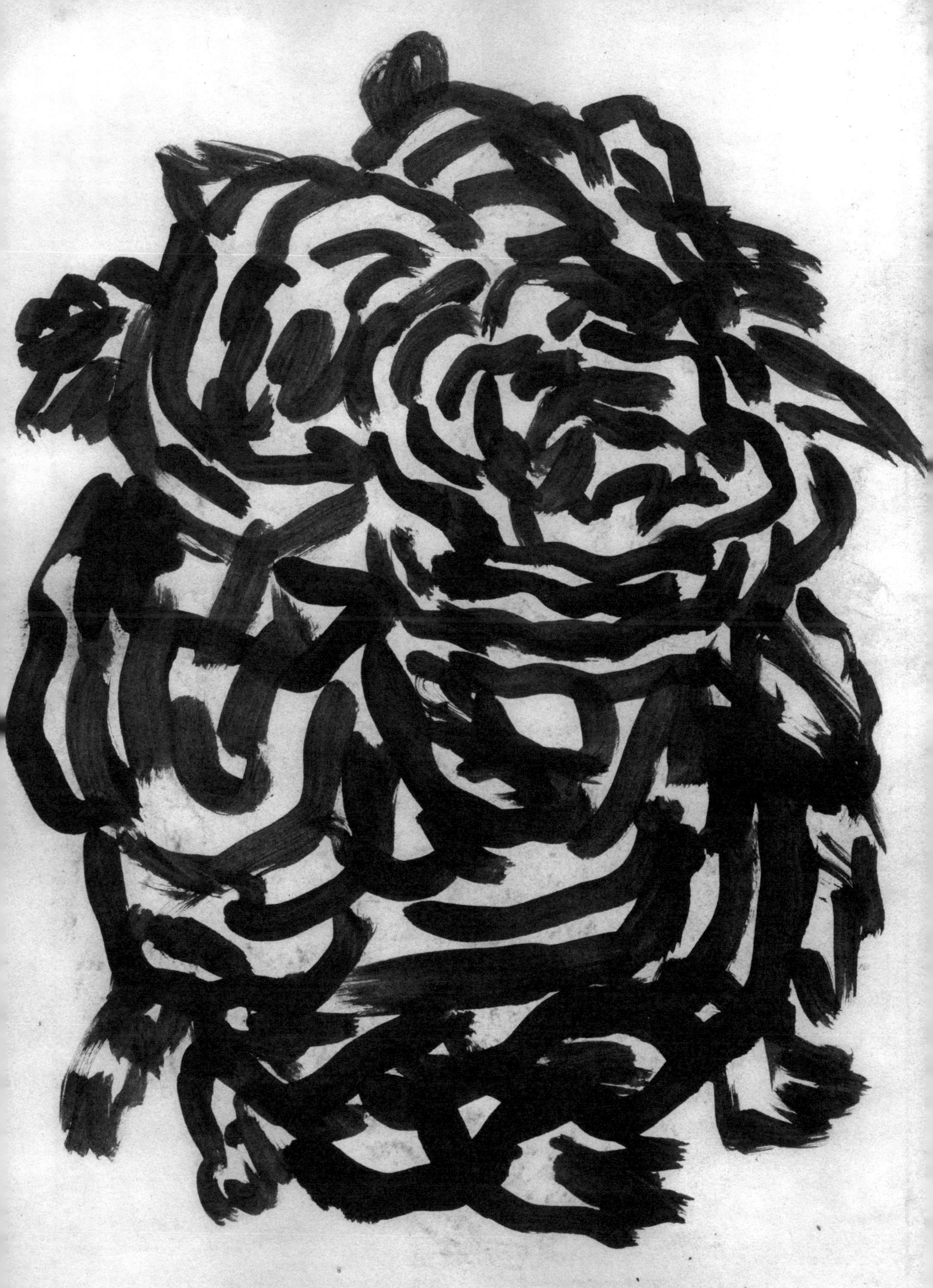

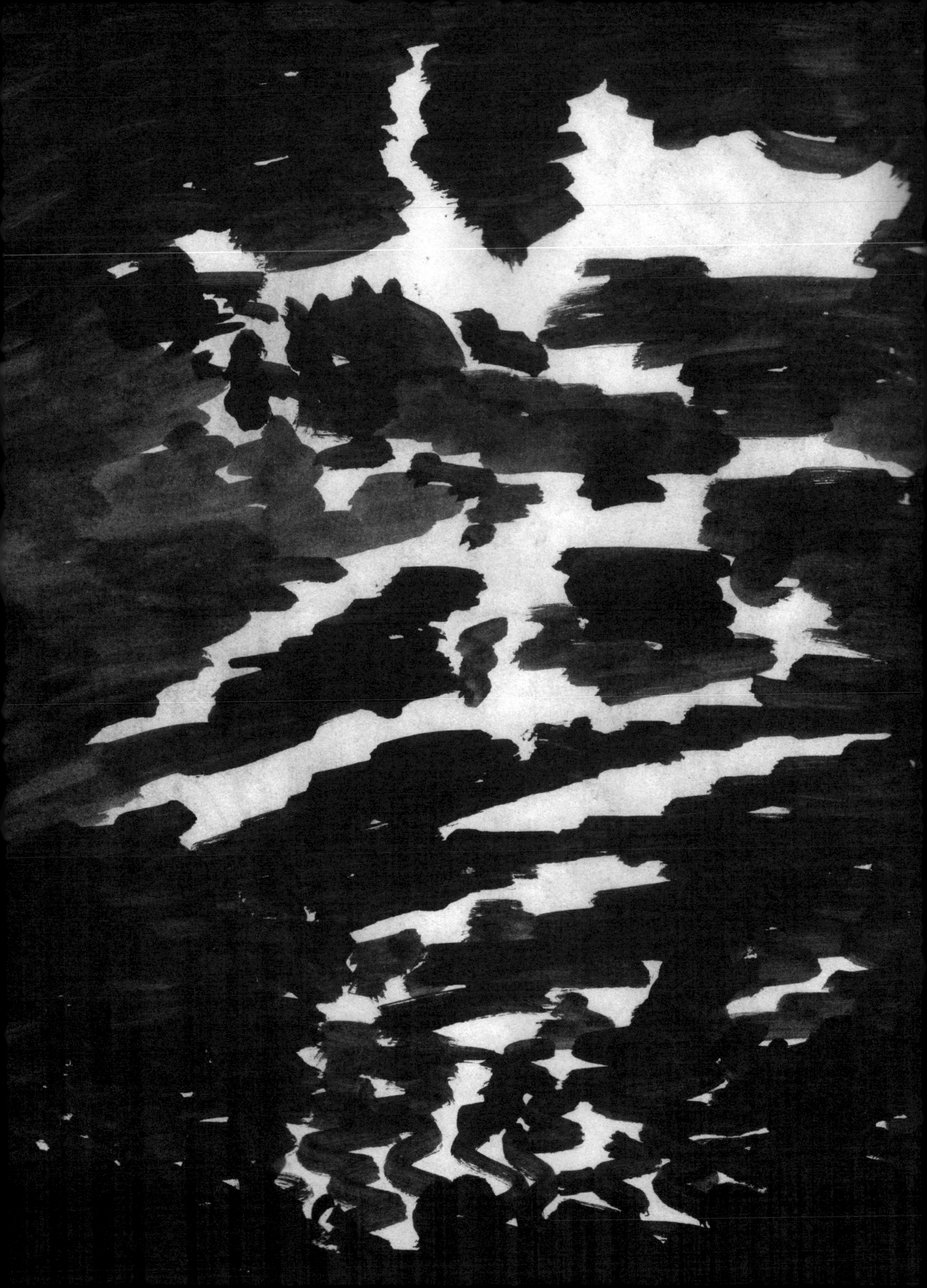

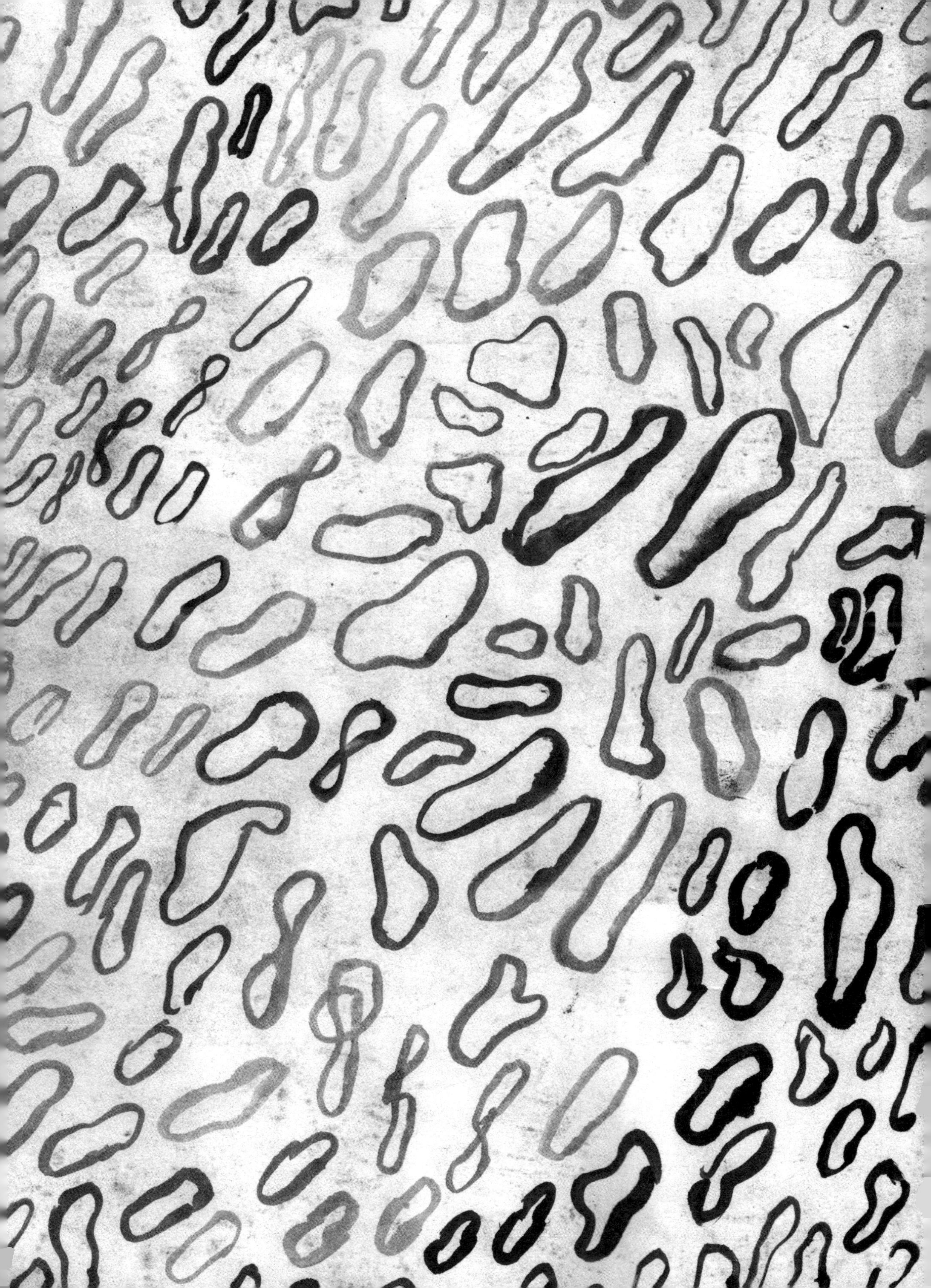

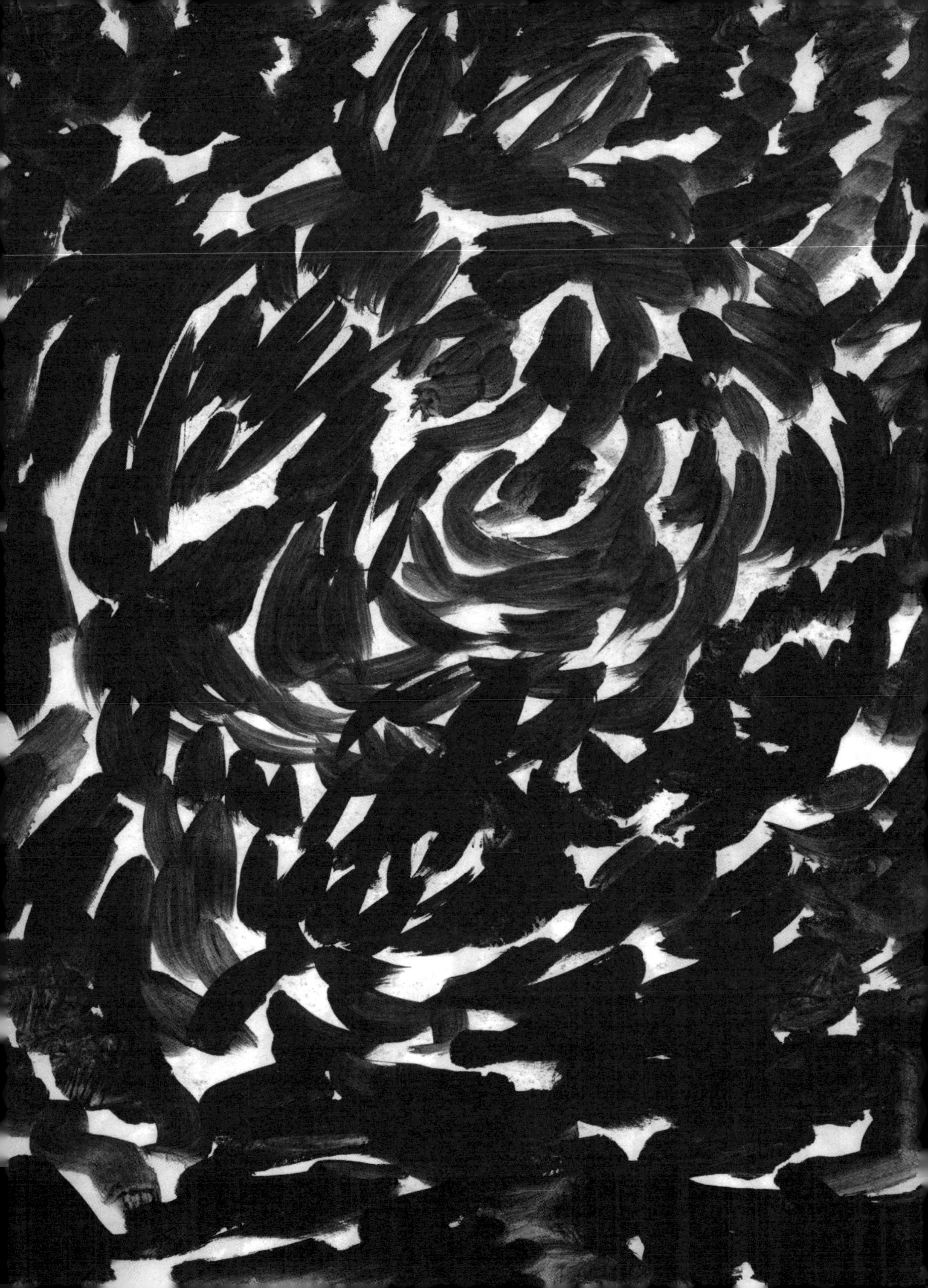

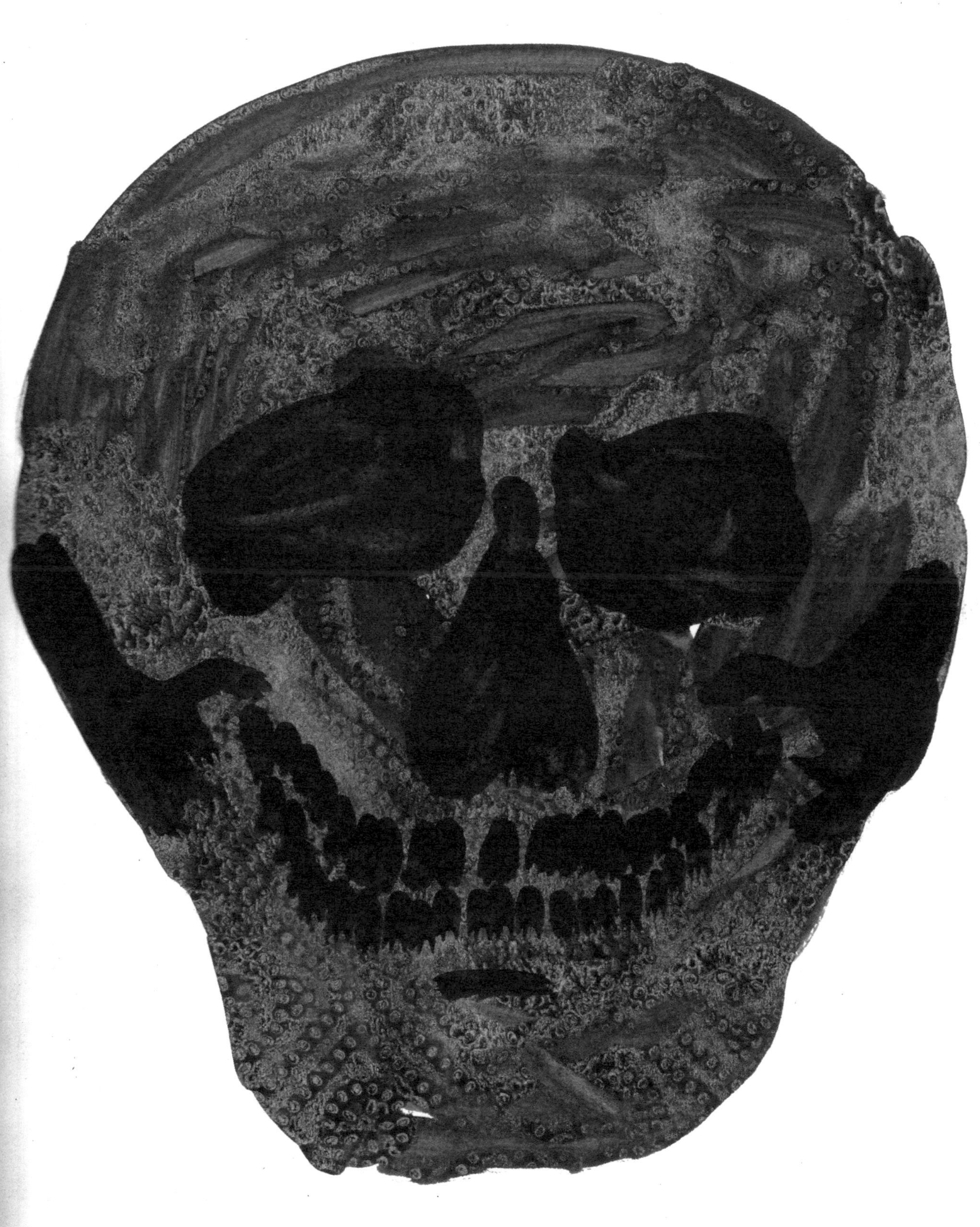

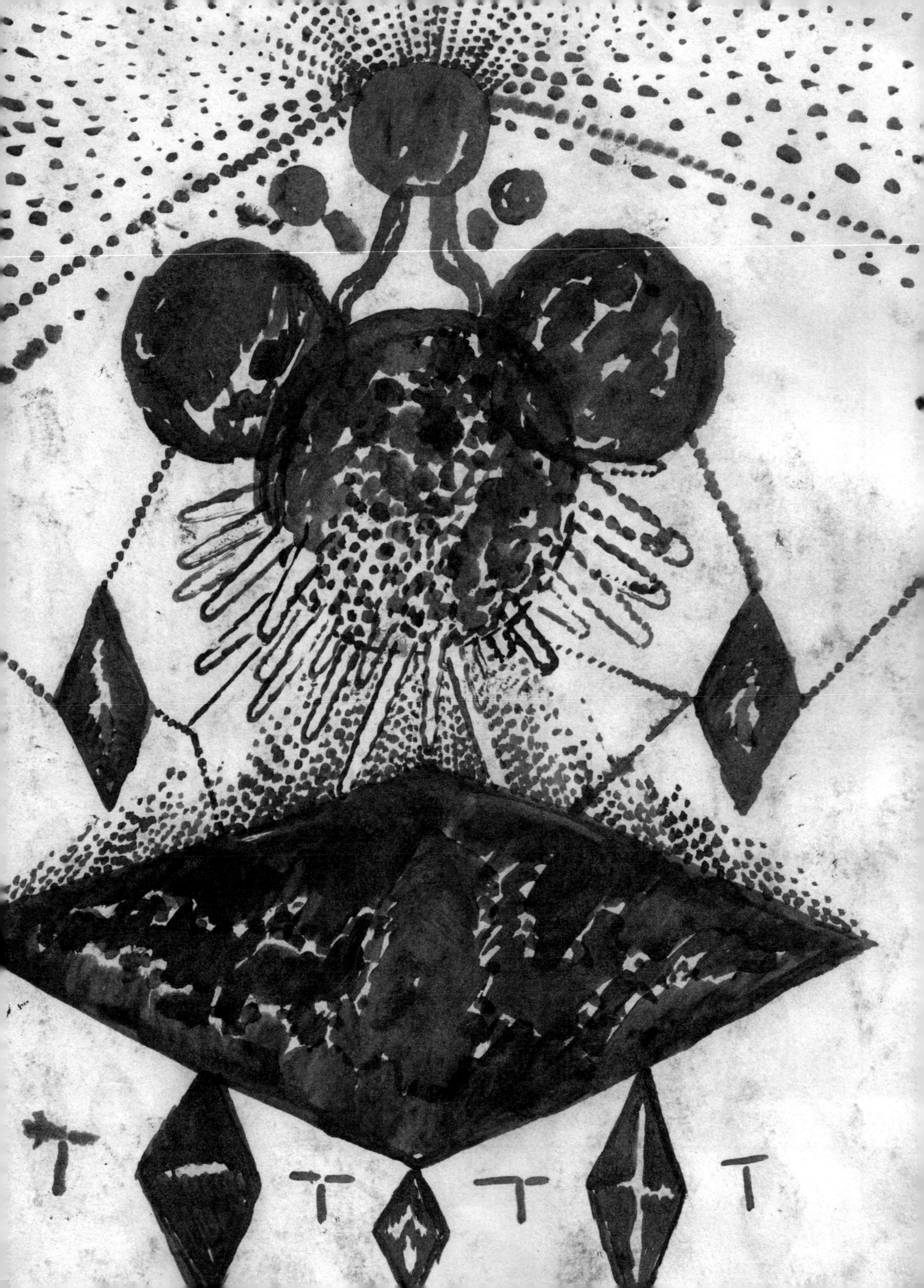

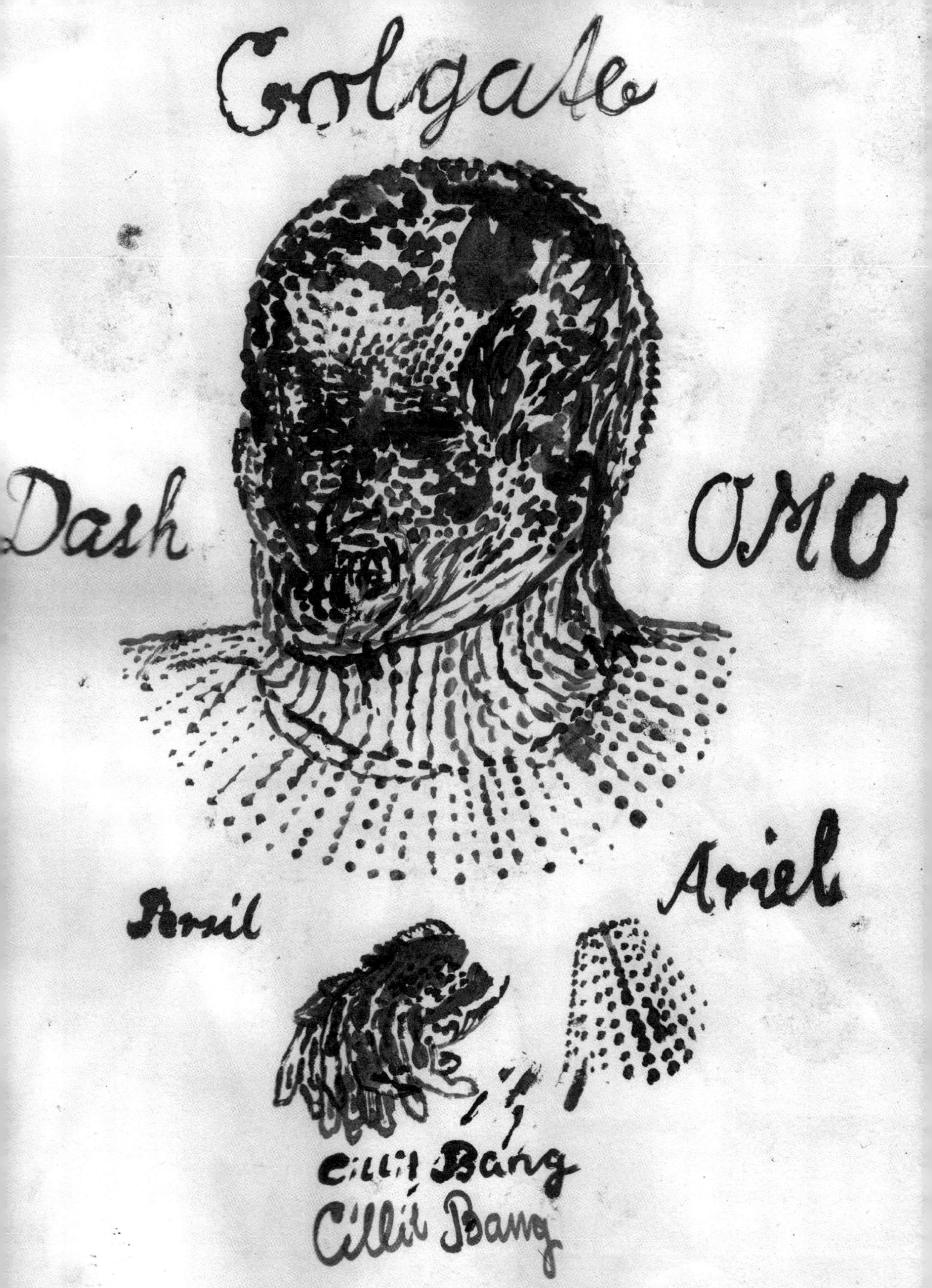

Colgate

Dash

OMO

Persil

Ariel

Cillit Bang

Cillit Bang

POL
DENN
SNACK
COLGATE SC

YGON

R

SNACK

HNIK-SCHNAK

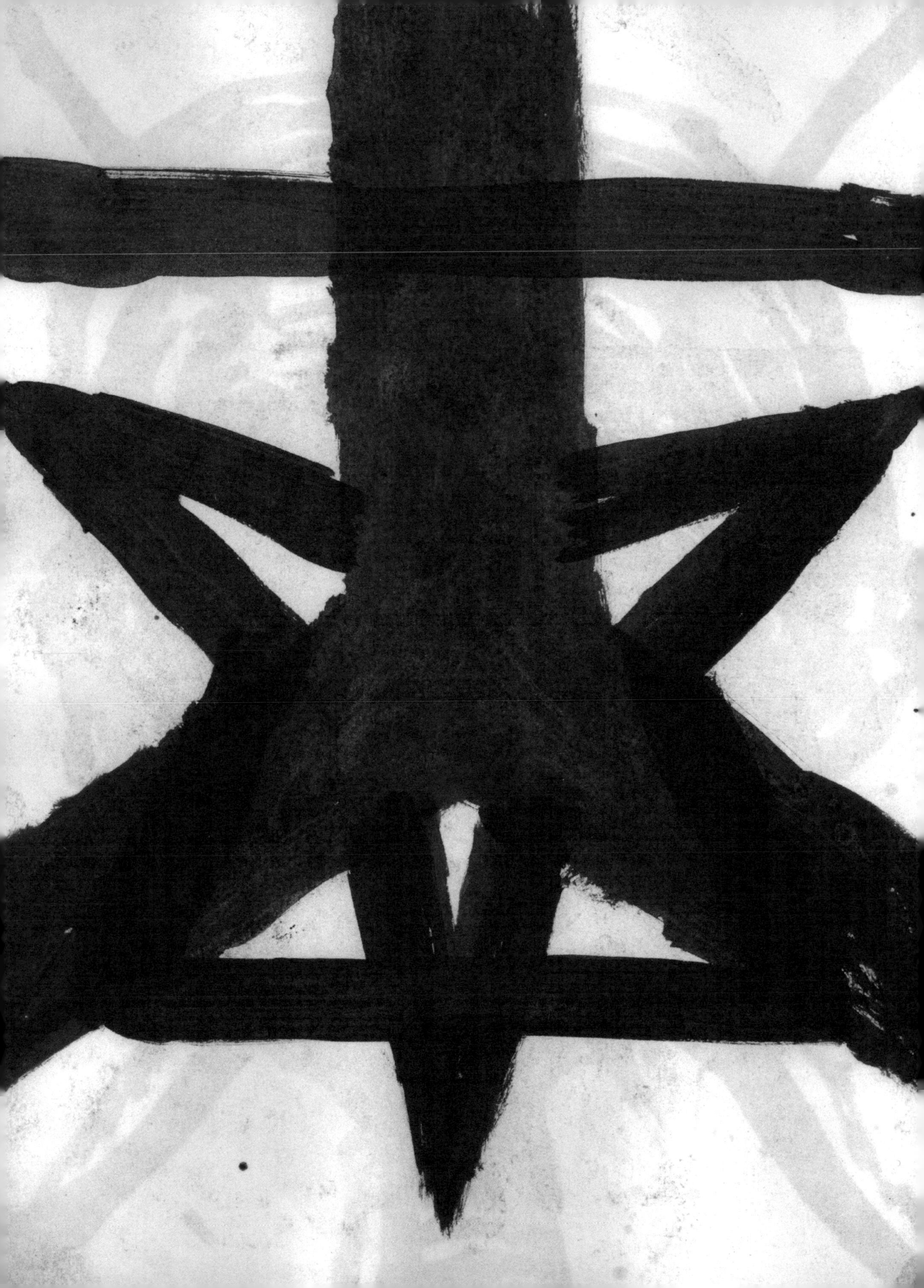

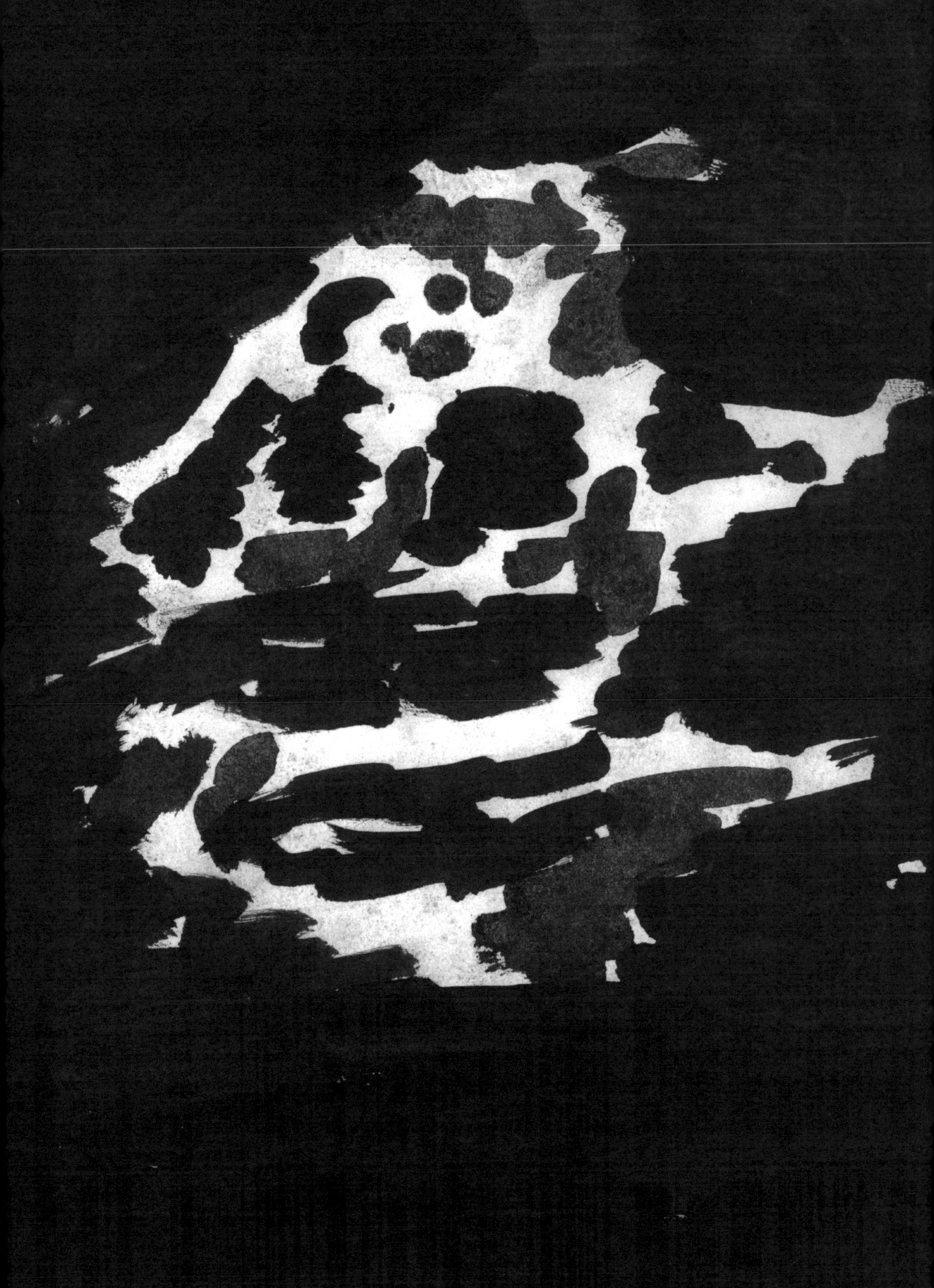

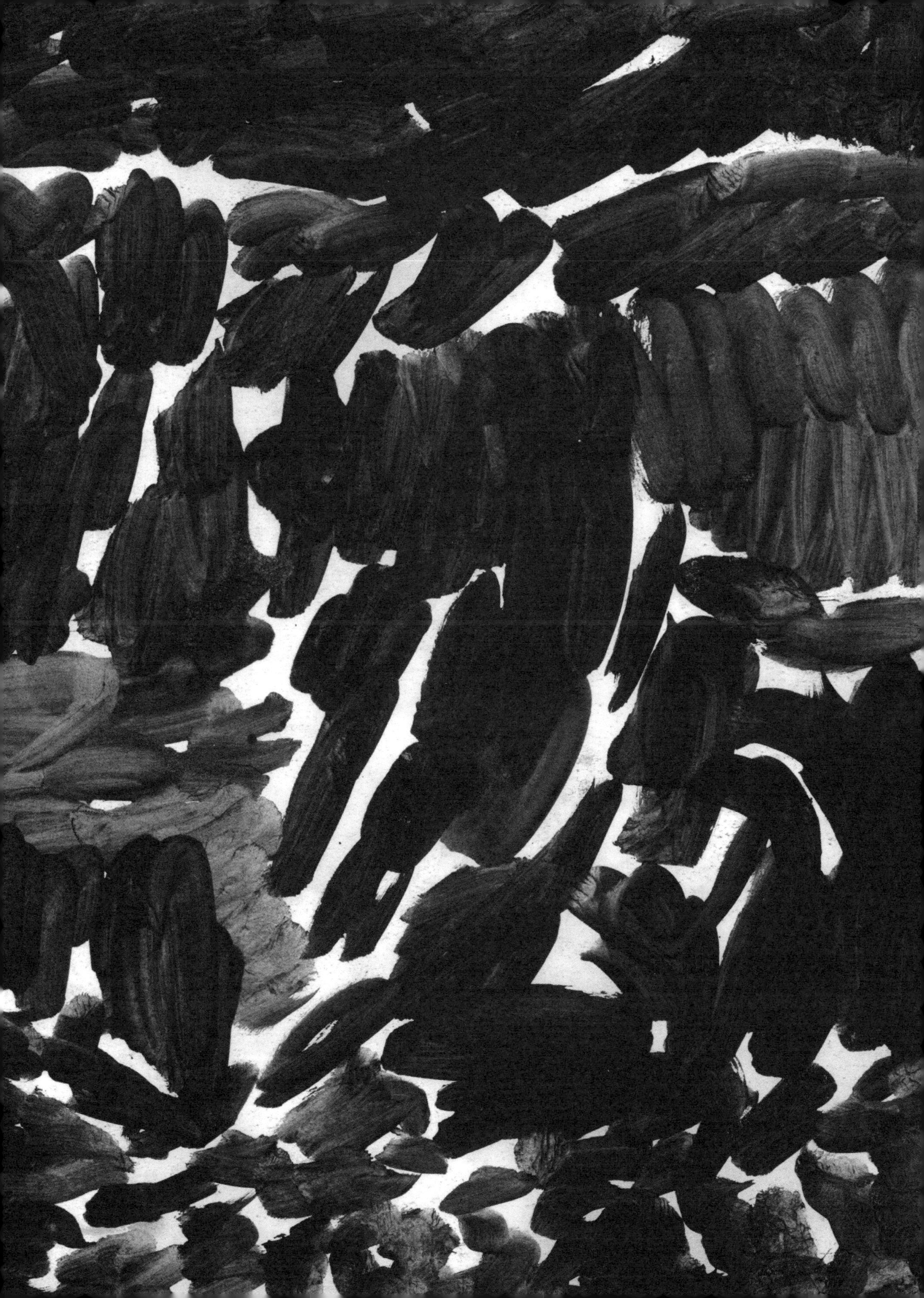

Black

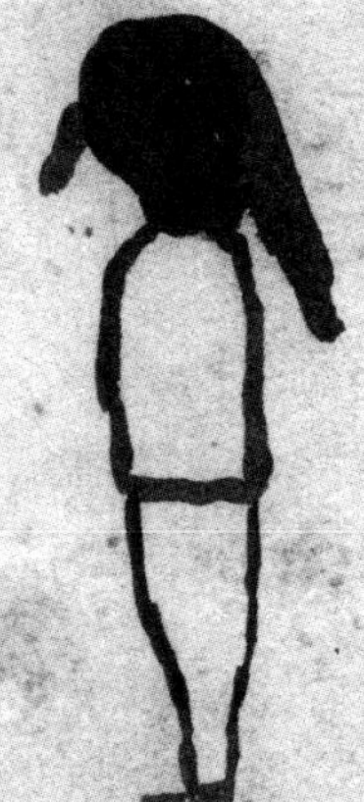

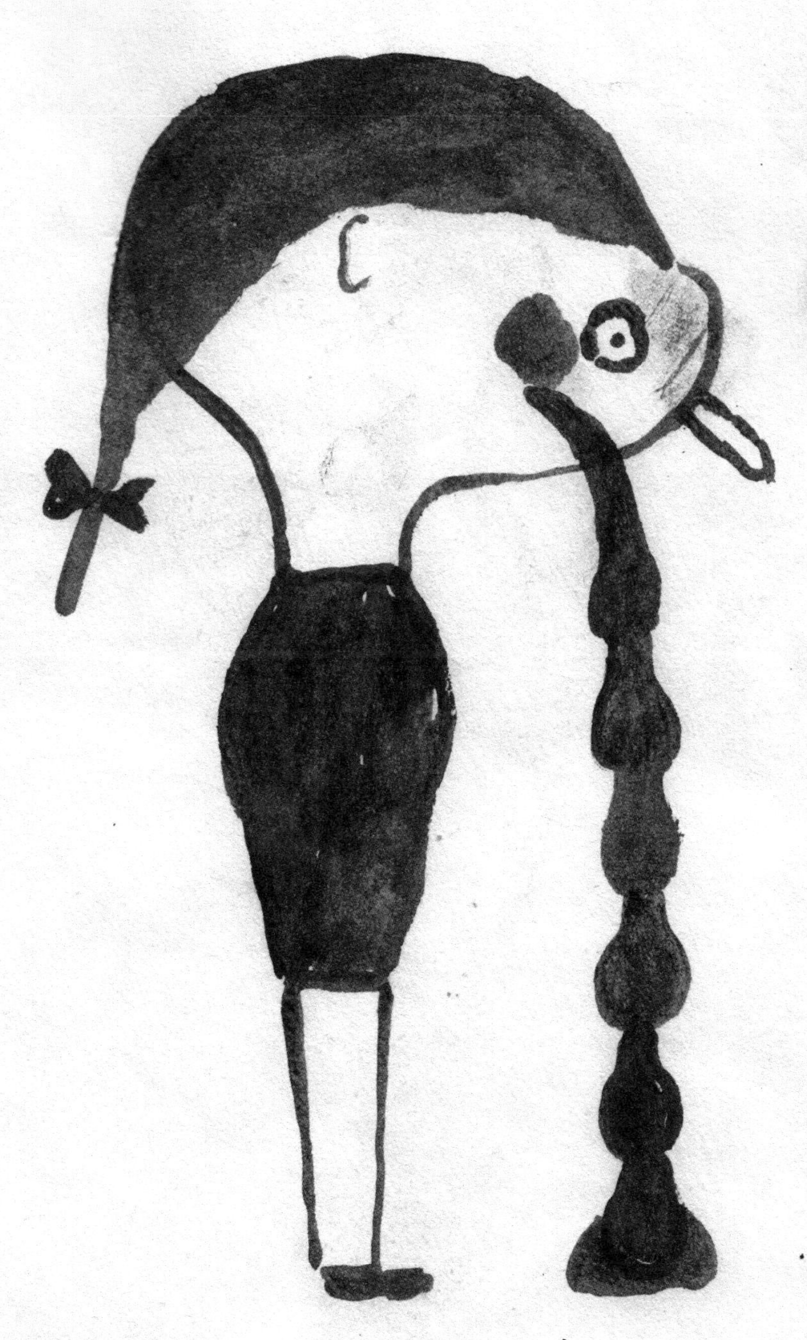

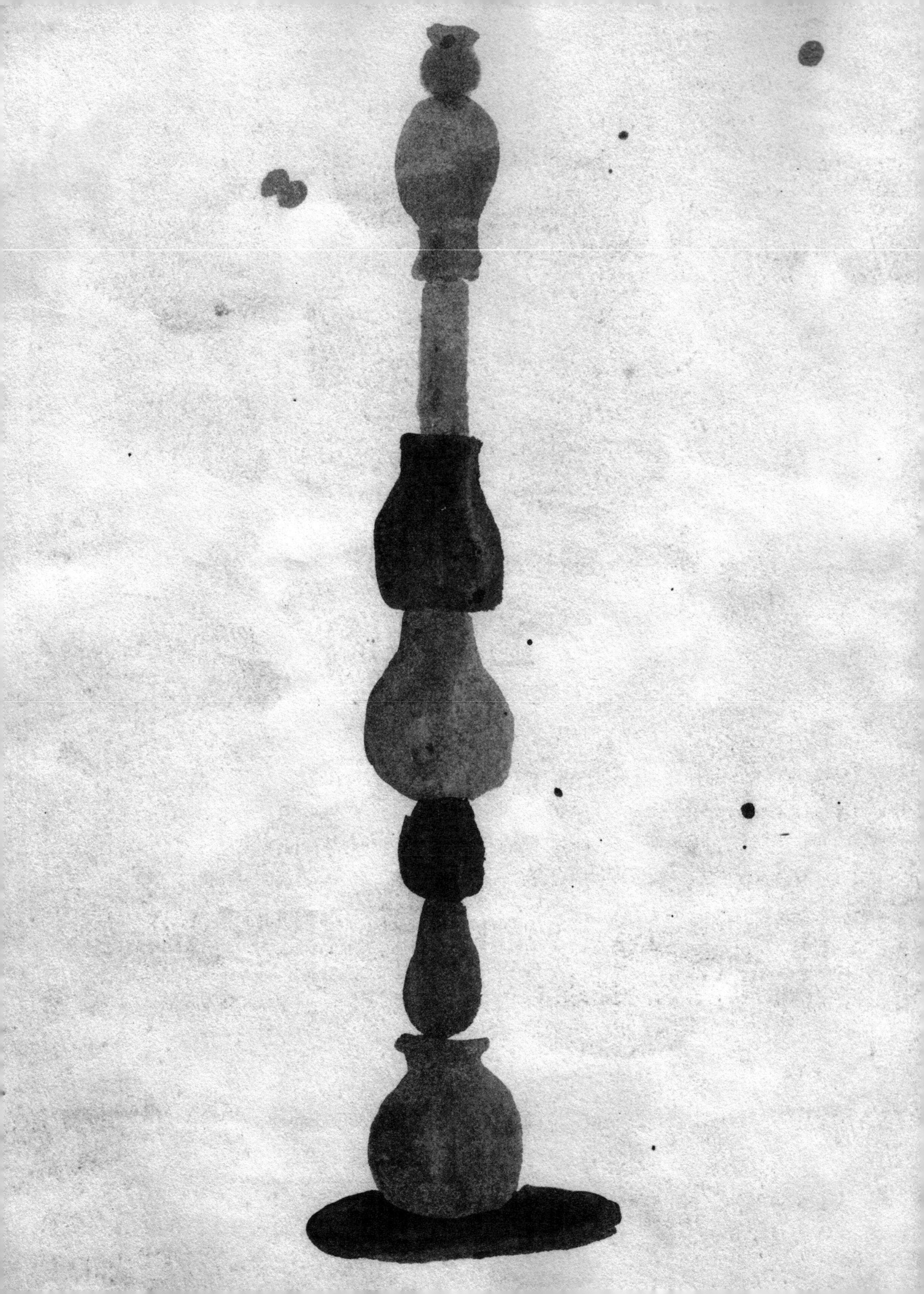

Dash

OMO

Cillit Bang

PERSIL

ARIEL

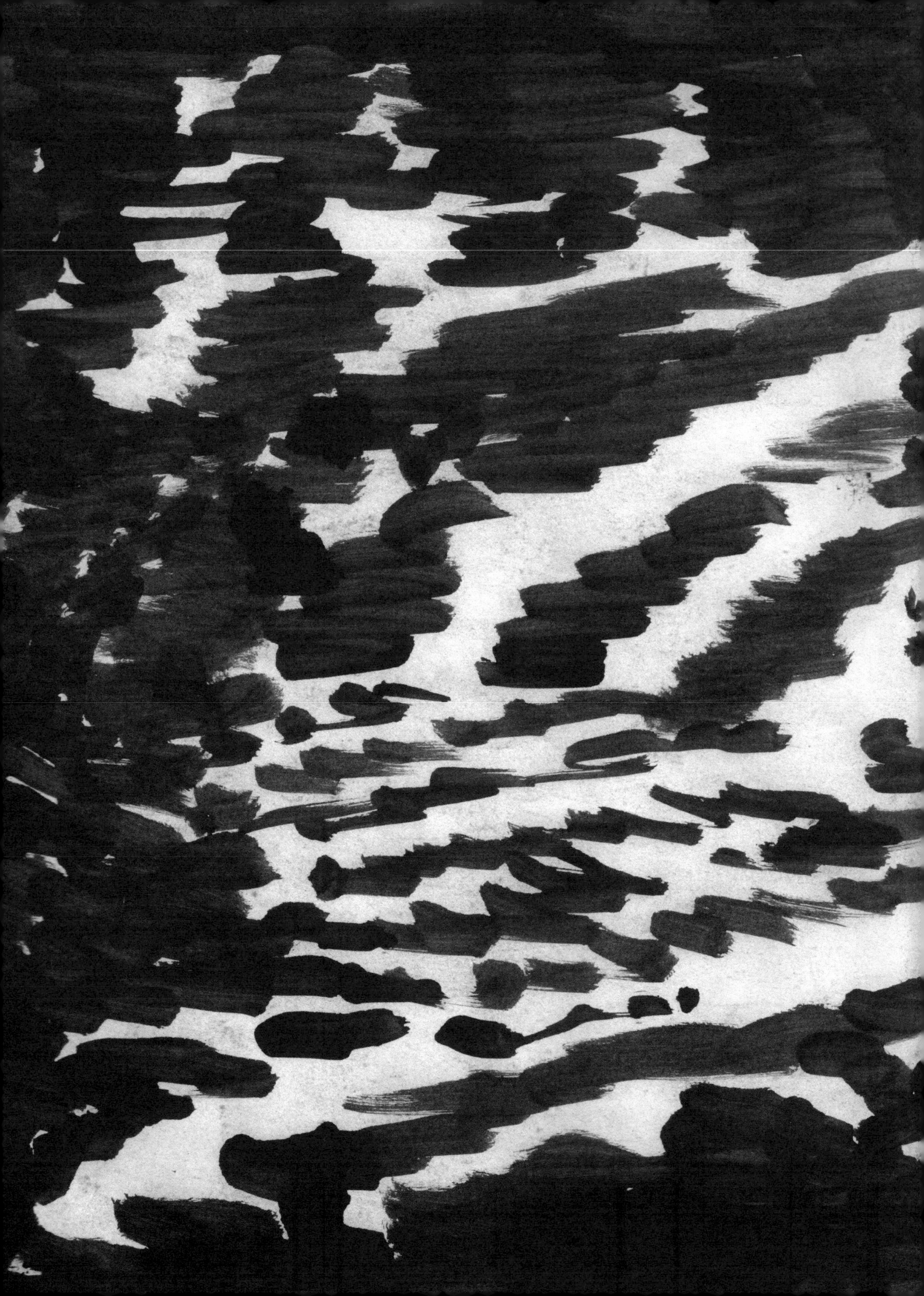

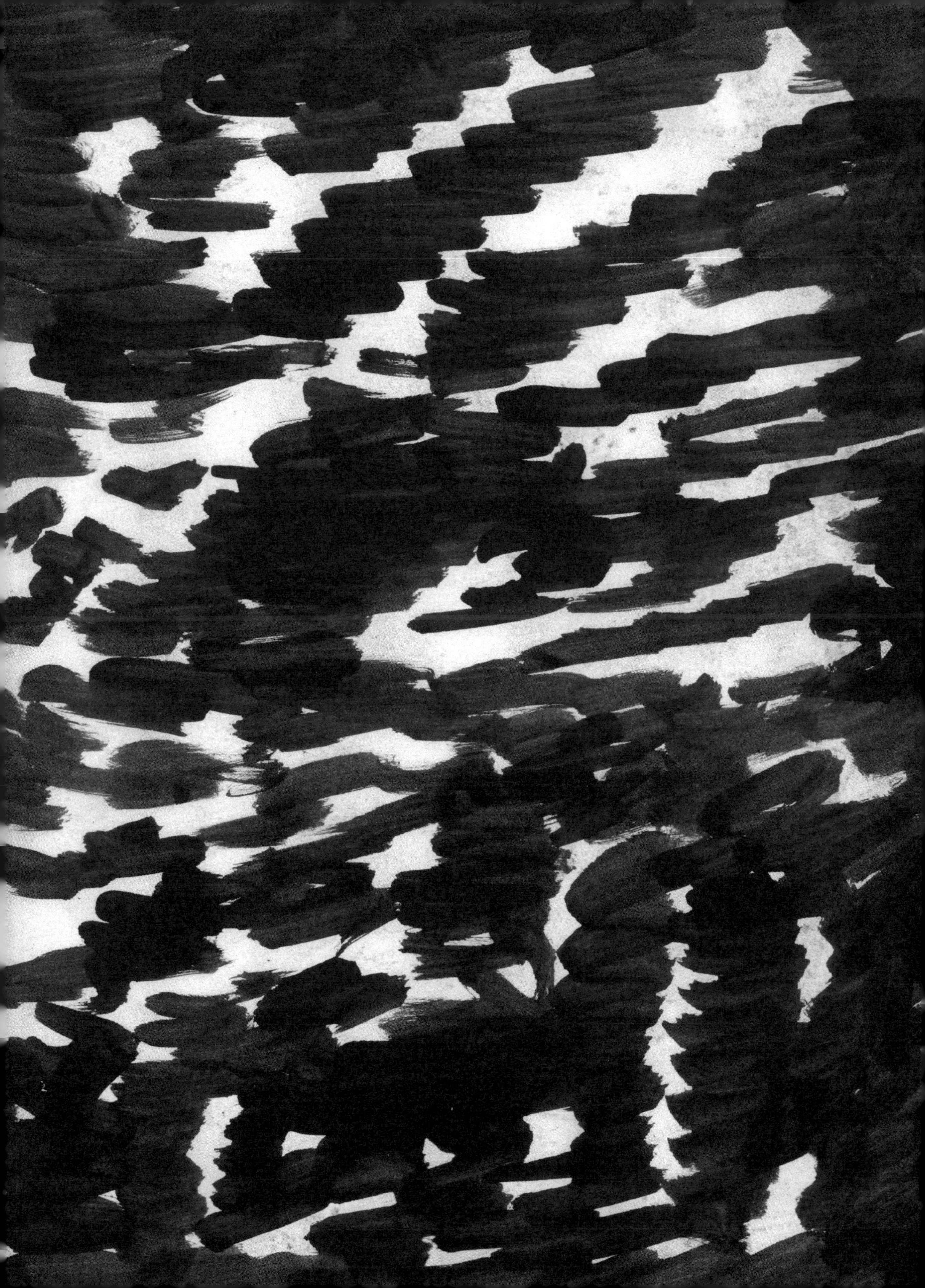

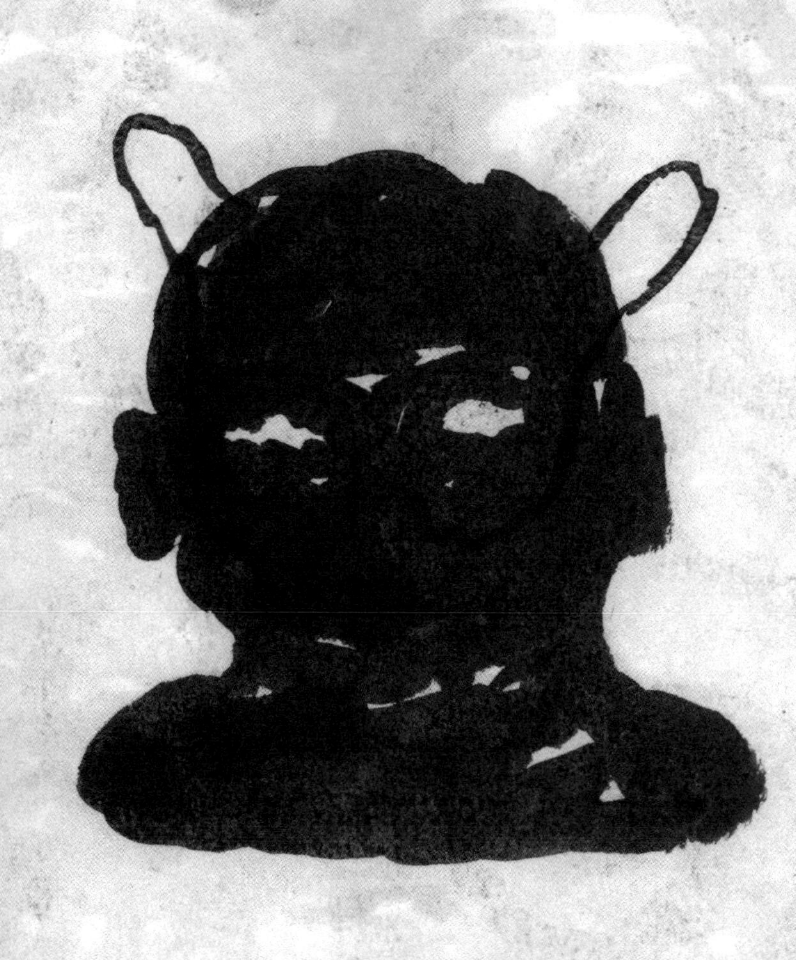

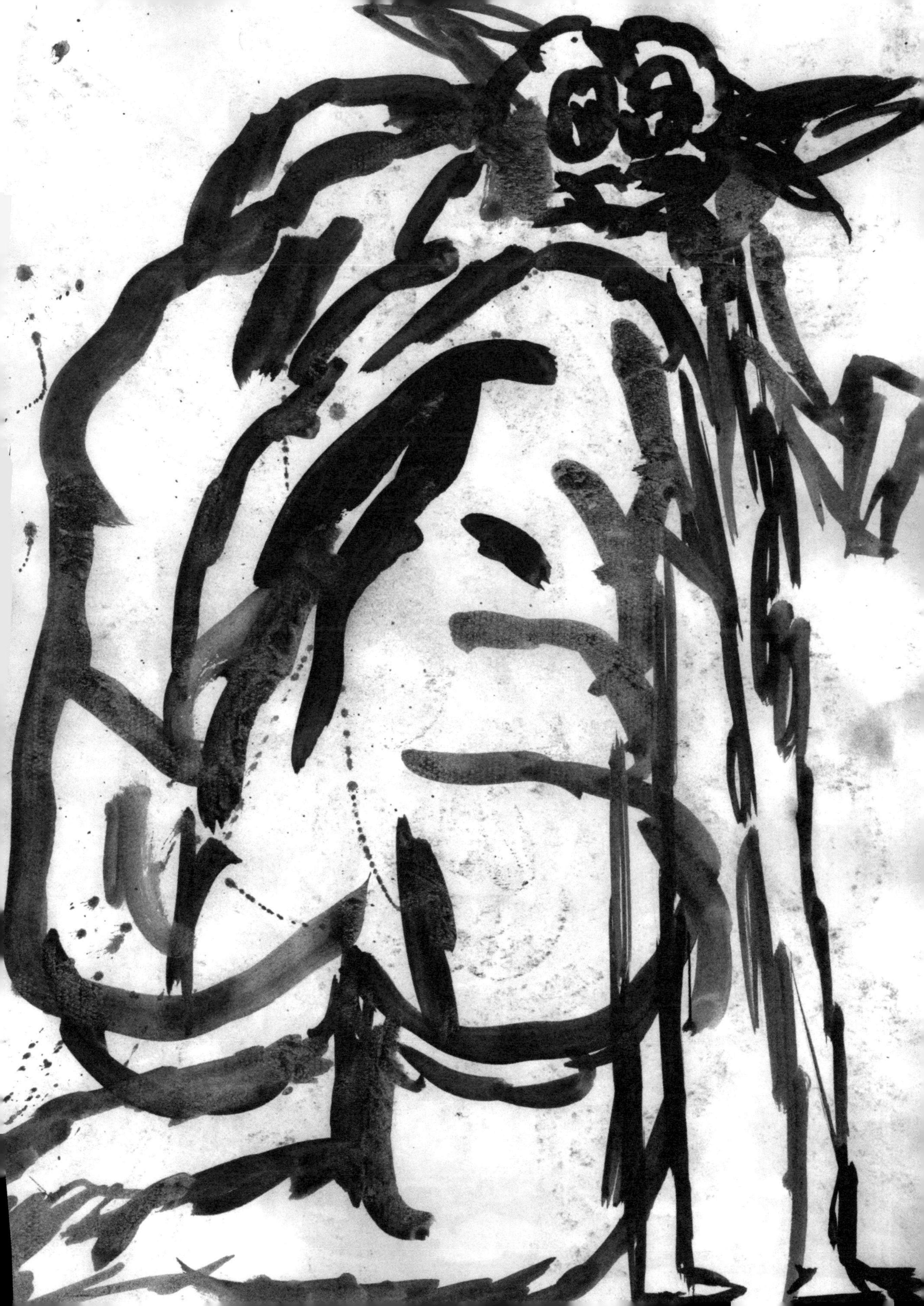

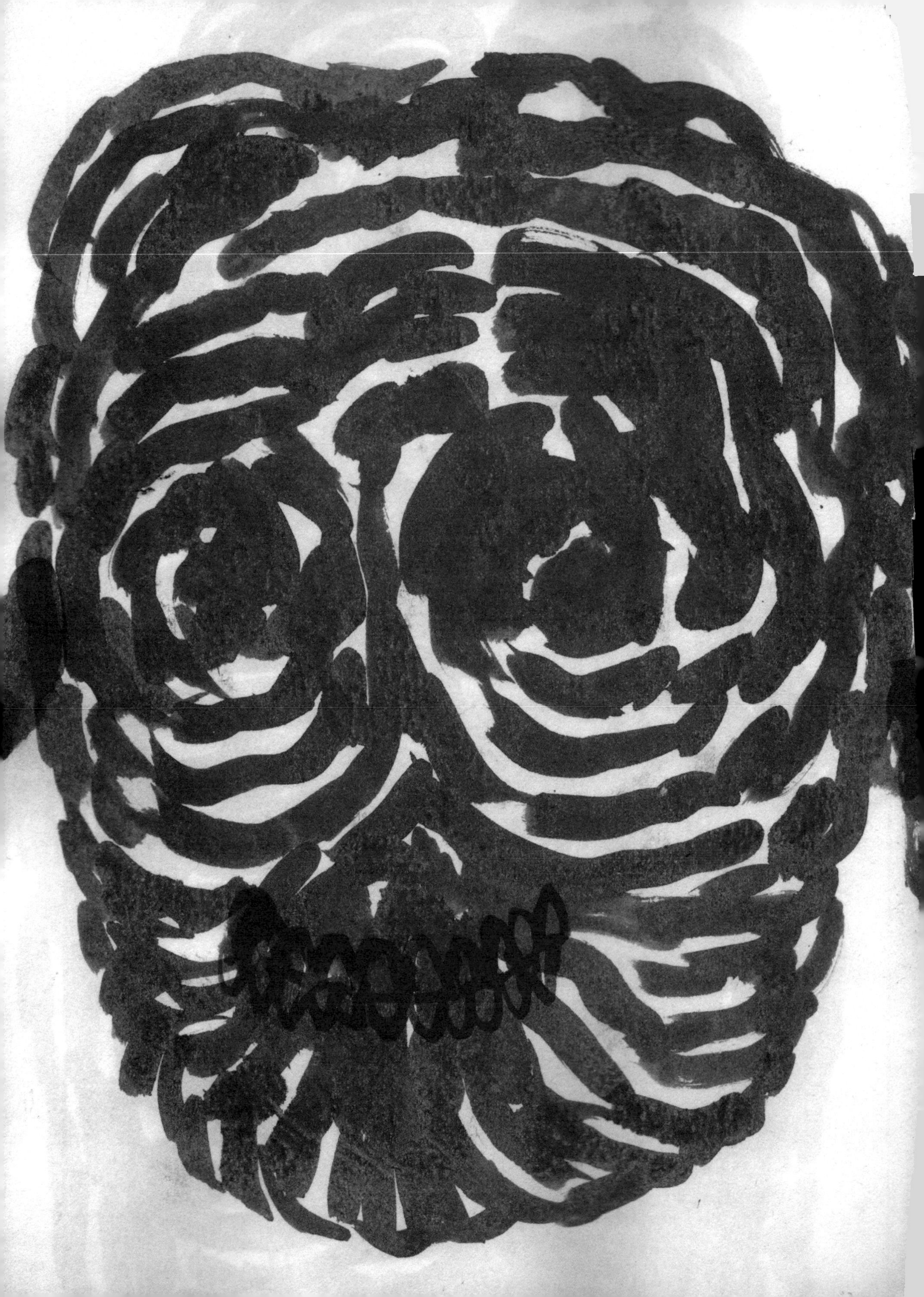